MYTH AND TRUTH
An Essay on the Language of Faith

MYTH AND TRUTH

An Essay on the Language of Faith

By

JOHN KNOX

THE UNIVERSITY PRESS OF VIRGINIA
Charlottesville

RICHARD LECTURES FOR 1963-64
University of Virginia

© *by the Rector and Visitors of the*
University of Virginia

THE UNIVERSITY PRESS OF VIRGINIA

First published 1964
Library of Congress Catalogue Card Number: 64-25858

FOREWORD

THIS small book comprises the lectures it was my privilege to give at the University of Virginia in the autumn of 1963 on the James L. Richard Foundation. The lectures were addressed to an audience consisting largely of university students and were prepared with such hearers in mind. No attempt has been made to revise the lectures radically, whether in form or substance; and they are here presented very much as they were originally delivered.

To Professor Lewis M. Hammond, chairman of the Richard Lecture Committee, and his colleagues I wish to express my appreciation of the honor of the invitation to give the lectures and of the many courtesies they showed me during my visit.

Thanks are given to two friends and academic associates, Dr. Olive Brose and Dr. Robert L. Horn, who were good enough to read my manuscript at an early stage in its development and to give me criticisms and suggestions which have been most useful. I am also grateful for the expert help of Miss Ann Belford, my research assistant at Union Theological Seminary in 1963–64.

JOHN KNOX

April 1964

CONTENTS

Foreword		v
One	The Problem of Faith and Truth	1
Two	Images and Myths	17
Three	Our Need of Myths	34
Four	Myth and History	51
Five	Myth, Legend, and Creed	65
Index		85

CHAPTER ONE

THE PROBLEM OF FAITH
AND TRUTH

WHAT are we to make of—and do with—the mythology which is so deeply embedded in the religious culture to which we belong? This is the very practical question with which we shall be concerned in this series of discussions. It probably does not need to be said that the religious culture I shall have principally in mind is the Christian culture which alone I know with any degree of intimacy. But the problems with which we shall be dealing are not essentially different for the Jew; and I shall hope that what I shall say will, in principle, seem relevant to Jew and Christian alike. To repeat, then, we shall be asking how we are to understand and deal with the mythological character of the religion we know.

To some of us—perhaps, in some measure, to all of us—it

may be shocking to hear Christianity, or Judaism, referred to as having a mythology at all. We have grown up associating myths exclusively with other religions, especially with the ancient pagan cults. Far from thinking of Christianity as being also in any sense or degree mythological, we have seen in its nonmythological character one of its principal distinctions and a decisive mark of its unique value and truth. Actually, however, even a little reflection will convince us that this distinction cannot be maintained. The biblical accounts of how God made the world and of how he will bring it to an end and other stories of his mighty acts cannot be separated, as regards the formal type or category to which they belong, from narratives on similar themes in Homer, in Virgil, or in Norse or German legend. If superiority in value or truth is to be found in the biblical stories, it will consist, not in the absence of the mythological, but in the particular character of the biblical mythology, and, more basically, in the superior value and truth of what is being expressed and conveyed through it. With these matters of value and truth we shall be concerned before this series of discussions has ended, but just now we are simply acknowledging the fact itself.

It will be obvious that in speaking thus I am presupposing a certain understanding of the word "myth." A recent writer speaks of myth as being "simply a numinous story";[1]

[1] Alan W. Watts, *Myth and Ritual in Christianity* (London: Thames and Hudson, 1953), p. 58. In a later publication (*The Two Hands of God* [New York: George Braziller, 1963], p. 2) Watts withdraws in effect the limiting word "story," indicating that "myth" must be thought of as including, not only narratives, but other expressions of the numinous as well. Neither now nor later shall I be attempting a formal definition of myth; but in this discussion a "myth" will always be a "story." It seems to

and Rudolf Bultmann, to whose important work on our theme we shall find ourselves referring later in this discussion, defines the word as "the use of imagery to express the otherworldly in terms of this world and the divine in terms of human life, the other side in terms of this side."[2] If the word is understood in some such way, it is obviously applicable to much in Bible and Creed; and it is in such a sense that I am using it—a human story of a divine action. But quite different understandings are possible. Sometimes the words "myth" and "mythology" are used in such close connection with primitive religion that their sense is entirely determined by this association. Archaic man's conceptions of nature and of God's immanence within it, his way of regarding time as cyclic rather than linear, and other characteristics of his mentality are made integral to the meaning of the words.[3] If it should be decided that they must be defined in this way, one would no longer be able to use them of the

---

me better to use another word—say, a broader term like "symbol"—for other numinous words or objects.

[2] "The New Testament and Mythology," in H. W. Bartsch (ed.), *Kerygma and Myth*, tr. R. H. Fuller (London: Society for the Promotion of Christian Knowledge, 1954), p. 10.

[3] This tends to be the case among historians of religion and anthropologists. If the essential meaning of the word "myth" is thought of strictly and exclusively in this way, one must either deny its applicability to the Hebrew-Christian materials or apply it in a very partial or "broken" sense. On this matter of whether the terms "myth" and "mythological" can appropriately be used of the biblical "stories," and in what sense, see M. Eliade, *Le mythe de l'éternal retour: Archétypes et répétition* (Paris: Librairie Gallimard, 1949); English translation by Willard R. Trask, *Cosmos and History: The Myth of the Eternal Return* (New York: Harper and Brothers, 1959), esp. pp. 95–162; and H. and H. A. Frankfort, *The Intellectual Adventure of Ancient Man* (Chicago: University of Chicago Press, 1946), esp. pp. 3–26 and 363–73. See also Joseph Campbell, *The*

biblical and credal materials with which we are concerned. But in that event we should need to find another word for the numinous stories we actually find in our tradition. Later I shall give some indications of the kind of numinous story I believe a biblical myth to be. Just now I am using the term in the broadest, most general, sense and am making the point that in this sense Judaism and Christianity, as certainly as other religions, have their myths and their mythologies.

We shall be the more ready to make this acknowledgment when we recognize, as on reflection we must, the necessity or inevitability of mythology. Religion could not exist without it. Theology is essentially—one may say, by definition—mythological, and this is as surely true of Christian theology as of any other. For the distinctively Christian message, the "gospel," is an announcement of something God has done—namely, of what he did in Christ—and distinctively Christian theology is concerned with explicating and communicating the concrete content, the realized inner meaning, of this divine act. It is an account of an action of God, and this is precisely what we are calling a myth. To be sure, the term suggests, not a plain, factual account, but rather a story or a picture—which means that the account is imaginative and therefore, to a degree at least, imaginary. But it is important

_____

Masks of God (New York: Viking Press, 1962), esp. the first several pages of the book.

The problem of how "myth" should be defined is a most difficult and complicated one, and, generally speaking, writers such as those I have just cited make no attempt at a comprehensive definition. See the opening pages of Watts, *The Two Hands of God*, already cited, and M. Eliade, *Myth and Reality* (New York: Harper and Row, 1963), pp. 5–6. "Is it even possible," Eliade asks, "to find *one* definition that will cover all the types and functions of myths in all traditional and archaic societies?"

to see that there cannot be such a thing as a plain, factual account of a divine act, whether among pagans, Jews, or Christians. One might conceivably make a purely logical or metaphysical definition of the word "God" or one might affirm the bare fact of God's reality without the use of any imaginary story or picture; but one could not go beyond such abstract statements and try to say something about any action of God, or about God's relation to the world, or about his concrete meaning for us without resort to mythological speech—that is, without employing images from our human experience which, by definition, cannot strictly or literally apply. We find ourselves speaking of God as "coming" or "going" or "sending" or "forming" or "building" or "battling" or "raising" or "casting down" or "ransoming" or "begetting," according as the nature of the particular story or picture requires or makes appropriate.

In a word, we find ourselves dramatizing or mythologizing. Use either of these terms you wish or find some other; but however you want to say it, the main point is clear and undeniable: we are no longer speaking factually or literally. We cannot speak so when we are speaking of God, for our speech can use only the terms provided by our human experience and thought, and God transcends both. The divine, however near to, even pervasive of, the human it may be, is still essentially transhuman or superhuman. To identify God with the world or with men is to deny his reality as God. To equate the divine with the human—even with the human in its deepest dimension—is to deny the distinctive existence of the divine. God's thoughts are not our thoughts and his ways are not our ways. This is not merely a fact about God; it belongs to his very nature as God that this should be true. The word "God" is emptied of all meaning unless this transcendence is affirmed. If, therefore, we would speak of God's being and nature, we must make use of analogy, interpreting him in categories which arise out of our reflection upon our own life; and if we would speak of any "action" of God, we shall perforce speak mythologically, God becoming, so to speak, a character in a story or drama, the terms of which are supplied by our experience with men and things.

This being the fact, how is the Christian to respond to it? What bearing does the recognition of it have upon his life as a Christian, and how is he to deal with it? It is with questions of this kind that these lectures are concerned. I shall make no effort at a comprehensive or systematic discussion of mythology, nor shall I be dealing with the subject as a psychoanalyst might, or an anthropologist, or a sociologist, or, for that matter, a historian of culture in the general sense. Even with regard to the biblical mythology, with which alone we shall be seriously engaged, I shall make no attempt to trace its cultural roots or to determine its relations with other ancient mythologies. In a word, I shall speak, not as the scientific historian of religion—although I shall often be dependent on his work and hope that I shall not in any way violate his findings—but as a Christian teacher concerned about the bearings of some of these findings on the life and thought of the Church. I repeat, then, the practical question with which we began: What is the Christian to make of the fact that many of his credal affirmations, many of his theological beliefs, are (in the broad, rather loose sense in which I have thus far used the term) mythological in character? Is he to regard it as an embarrassing fact which he must grudgingly concede? Is it a fact which, as he must see it, can have only the effect of confirming the denials of the atheist or the doubts of the skeptic and of making religious faith more difficult? Or, on the contrary, is it to be seen as a liberating fact, a means of both releasing and enriching religious faith, and therefore to be eagerly welcomed and warmly embraced? I am sure we ought to regard it in the latter way, and I shall be greatly disappointed if, in the course of these discussions, we are not led to think of it so, if we do not already. First, however, we need to say something of a more general kind about the relation of faith to truth. In doing so we shall not be speaking specifically about myths and mythology, but we shall be laying a foundation for our whole discussion.

When I referred a moment ago to the possibility that the Christian may feel an aversion to recognizing that his religion has anything to do with mythology, or mythology with his religion, I know that I said nothing strange or surprising. We should expect him to react in this way, and perhaps we feel something of the same aversion ourselves. This is partly owing to a misunderstanding of the nature of mythology, and this we shall try to deal with later. But it is not unlikely in any given instance that the hostility or apprehension we feel over this particular matter may have a broader base in a more or less habitual attitude of mind toward man's scientific and philosophical work and to the facts and truths which it has brought, or may bring, to light. We shall not go into the historical or other reasons for it, but can we deny the fact that Christians have often found themselves taking this negative, or at any rate distrustful, attitude? Insofar as this has been the case, the Church in its relation to the intellectual enterprise of mankind has been constantly on the defensive—and, one must add, on the run—feebly resisting at first what in the end it has been forced abjectly to yield to. This began to be true certainly as early as Copernicus, and you and I have witnessed the same process at work in our own time.

It is hardly necessary to refer to the tragic effects of this negative attitude or stance on both the Church itself and the larger society. For the Church it has meant not only a measure of alienation from the intellectual community but also a stifling of its own intellectual life. Its efforts to understand itself and its distinctive task in the world have been arbitrarily limited. An intolerable and paralyzing tension has been set up between the religious and the intellectual spheres within the minds of generations of Christians, upon whom has been laid an obligation to believe what their minds have found incredible. As for society as a whole, this same divisive and alienating process has undoubtedly contributed to that drying up of the deepest springs of our cultural life which we call "secularization" and which, like a kind of dry rot, threatens to destroy both our society and our souls. For man cannot indefinitely live on the surface of things; he must feel firmness in the depths below him. It would be a gross oversimplification to attribute the modern trend toward secularization to any one factor. But surely one important cause has been the Church's inability to respond positively and creatively to many of the facts which man's scientific and philosophical inquiry has established as unquestionably true.

This situation is utterly anomalous and quite unwarranted. It does not need to be. Indeed, an egregious denial of the essential nature of religious faith is involved in it. How incredible that we should be under obligation to believe the incredible! How impossible that we should be asked to credit the impossible, or to reject by an act of will what our minds find it necessary to accept! And how monstrous the conception of a God who would impose such a demand! If anyone is to be anti-intellectual, we shall not expect it to be one who ascribes our minds, along with whatever else belongs to our essential nature as men, to an ultimate divine Goodness. If anyone might be expected to welcome every newly discovered fact about the world and about human life, it would be one who trusts, adores, and rejoices in the Creator of all things. If anyone is in position never to fear truth, it would seem to be the one who loves God—who, however else He is thought of, must be the ultimate Source and Norm of truth. And yet, although the Church has always known this in its heart, it has over and over again fallen into the trap of identifying religious faith with the acceptance of certain facts and propositions and the rejection of others, and has thus gratuitously placed itself at the mercy, so to speak, of scientific or philosophical inquiry, wistfully hoping that its own precious facts and propositions will be vindicated but deeply fearful that they will not be—and often with good reason.

The truth is that religious faith is not a matter of accepting or rejecting facts with which the scientist is concerned or of believing or denying propositions with which the philosopher is dealing. Religious faith is an awareness of the depths in our existence and a certain kind of response to what reveals itself in them. These depths are there—are there, not only for confessing Jews or Christians or Muslims or Hindus, but for every man. Because one may feel them as emptiness or nothingness, one may seek to escape the reality of them by occupying oneself with various superficial concerns. But such efforts at diversion must finally fail and can never, even for a moment, be fully successful. A. N. Whitehead has written that religious experience begins with "God the Void";[4] we all know him so even if we never come to know him in any other way. It is possible to come to know him also as Love; but when we thus confess him, we are not stating either a fact which our scientific research has discovered (or might conceivably disprove) or a proposition which logical or philosophical analysis has established (or might conceivably refute). Rather, we are simply describing the way we have come to feel the depths within and beneath our existence, the way they have disclosed themselves to us.[5]

Nor is faith an alternative or competing route to such facts or propositions. Faith is not a way of learning facts or of arriving at sound formulations of the structures of being or thought. Faith is not a kind of short cut to truth, a bypassing of intellectual effort. It is often thought of so. We

[4] *Religion in the Making* (New York: Macmillan Company, 1926), p. 16.

[5] I say "within and *beneath*" because transcendence (in some direction, so to speak) needs to be affirmed of God. This is a point which is not made quite clear, I think, in certain parts of J. A. T. Robinson's book, *Honest to God* (Philadelphia: Westminster Press, 1963), a book with whose intention, as I understand it, I am in sympathy. Many of us have been greatly helped by Paul Tillich's emphasis upon the dimension of depth, and my indebtedness to him in what I am now writing will be apparent. It will not do, however, to identify God with the "depths" in man, although it may be recognized that God meets or finds us there. It is *out* of the depths that we cry to God (Ps. 130:1). This is true even if God is apprehended as "deeper" still, a Depth beneath our own.

suppose, for example, that faith gives us answers to historical questions. (We cannot establish by historical evidence this or that occurrence; but, we say, we accept it on faith.) Or we suppose that faith can furnish us with final and indubitably true propositions about God and his ways with men, even though our own minds find the propositions unintelligible or incredible. (This or that proposition makes no sense to us; but we believe it, as we say, by faith.) Now in both of these cases we are using a good word "faith" to cover our lack of seriousness about what is true, just as we often use the good word "grace" to cover our lack of seriousness about what is just. Faith gives us no answers to questions either about historical or other scientific facts or about philosophical or theological concepts. Unless the application of our own minds, our intelligence and imagination, to the actual materials furnished us in our experience, including our experience as religious persons, brings us the answers to such questions, we simply do not have them.

The truth of the matter is that faith gives us no answers to *any* questions. It is our answer to God; it is not God's answer to our questions. It is our recognition of and response to the ultimate divine reality which has disclosed itself within our experience. Faith, then, is a kind of knowledge—and indeed the surest kind of knowledge there is, the knowledge of concrete reality, the knowledge that consists in immediate awareness. Sometimes faith has been thought of as a venture, a betting on what is recognized to be only a possibility, a risking of one's life on the hypothesis of God's reality. I used to speak in this way sometimes but can no longer find this kind of language quite true. This is not because I am less often assailed by doubt or tempted to despair, but rather because I would no longer define such moments of uncertainty and inner struggle as moments of faith. For faith is the experience of being grasped by God's indubitable reality, the actual knowing of him by whom we are fully known, the actual resting in him who made us for himself.

And the facts and concepts of various kinds? I no more learn them in the moment of faith than, in the moment when my friend opens his heart to me, I learn where he was born, or who his parents were, or acquire a sound theory about the structure of personality. With facts and concepts revelation does not provide me—whether it be the revelation of my friend or the revelation of God. In the moment of revelation we are confronted by One of whom we do not dare ask any questions but who has his own question to ask, "Lovest thou me?" Faith is not believing what we have good reason for knowing is not true (as though we really could!); it is not *believing* something at all, whether a fact or a proposition. It is not getting answers to our questions; it is making answer to God's question: "Yea, Lord, thou knowest that I love thee."

Such faith casts out all fear except the fear of God—which is only another way of speaking of our response to the ultimate truth and its claim on us. For what is the "fear of God" but awe before that which infinitely transcends us both in value and in depth and fullness of being, solemn wonder that this Transcendence should speak and be present in our own hearts, and dread lest, by living as though life were a small and tawdry thing, we betray both God and our real selves? Nothing else, or not otherwise, shall we fear. Least of all shall we fear truth, truth of whatever kind or order.

In one of the prayers of Milner-White we are led to ask that God shall give us "such trust" in truth that we shall "ask no rest from its demands and have no fear in its service."[6] But the strange fact is that some of us find ourselves fearing truth because we love the very God to whom we address such a prayer, while others of us feel forced to deny God because we love the very truth he bids us trust. Some reject truth without knowing they are rejecting God. Others love truth without knowing it is God they love. On neither side is the passionate concern for truth recognized as the essentially religious thing it is. The Church must bear some part of the blame that this is so.

I have just said "some *part* of the blame"; for responsibility for the tragic conflict between science and faith does not rest on the Church alone. It would not do to identify the difference between the two as the difference between love of truth, on the one side, and distrust of truth, on the other. Actually, religion has been as devoted to truth as science—has always professed to be and, at its best, has always been. The trouble is that the "truth" which it has sought and prized has been a different "truth" from that which science has sought and prized; and neither religion nor science has fully come to terms with the "truth" of the other. Neither, in other words, has found a way fully to recognize the richness and manifoldness of truth.

As a matter of fact, in this respect science is likely to be more ignorant and naïve than religion. The fact that its

[6] Eric Milner-White, *A Cambridge Bede Book* (New York: Longmans Green and Company, 1936).

"truth" is readily and neatly demonstrable and often has an immediate and obvious practical utility can easily betray science into a false complacency, which religion, at any rate in the modern world, is not likely to feel. The religious mind can hardly be as ignorant of, or as lacking in respect toward, what we call "scientific truth," as the scientific mind can so easily be as regards what may for convenience be called "religious truth." Actually, the scientific mind would be at least as much confounded and perplexed in accommodating itself fully to the truth revealed in religious experience (if it should see the need of trying to do this) as the religious mind is in accommodating itself to the truth disclosed in scientific research (as it cannot help seeing it must try to do). In a word, neither science nor religion sees truth in perfect focus; but because science looks with a single eye (that is, with one eye closed), it can more easily be deceived into thinking that it does.

This partial blindness of science is another way of referring to its inability to deal with the existential depths of man's life. Science is, by definition, concerned with the objective; it must observe its object from outside it. The great worth of science consists in its marvelous success in doing this, its amazing and ever-growing effectiveness in discovering, measuring, and thus to a degree controlling the objective world. Its temptation is to assume that all reality is objective, that one can stand outside everything that really exists and define and measure it. But actually, of course, this is not true. There is a whole world of reality that cannot be exhaustively investigated in this—or indeed in any other—way. One knows it from within it; and when one puts oneself outside it in order to look at it, it no longer stands by to be looked at. It has vanished from our sight; it has refused to be reduced to the status of an object to be measured and controlled. But this does not mean that it is not really there. Existential reality is *reality;* and the truth about it is *truth.* The science which recognizes its own inability to understand and describe this truth is simply acknowledging the limitations of its own proper field. But the science which assumes that what it cannot understand and describe cannot be truth at all is self-deceived and falls as far short of being true science as the religious faith which pretends to a knowledge of objective facts of all kinds falls short of being true faith.

I have been speaking of "religion" and "science," sometimes as though they were discrete essences of some kind and sometimes as though the terms stood for two distinct classes of men. Needless to say, neither of these ways of speaking, or thinking, is true. Both terms designate aspects of the response to life and the world which all men make, as individuals and as cultural groups. Any conflict between "science" and "religion," between "reason" and "faith," is a conflict, not so much among us, as within us. We seem at times to be in danger of succumbing either to the superficiality, the false simplicity, of scientism or positivism, or to the obscurantism of a specious faith. The Christian not infrequently finds himself forced to come to terms with two "truths" which, according to all appearances, do not agree with each other. Where, he asks, is the unity, the inner coherence, of truth? How can the believer acknowledge fully the truth of reason, as he wants to do and indeed cannot help doing, without denying the truth revealed in the existence of the Church and in his own existence as a Christian, which, again, he wants to affirm and indeed cannot help affirming? How can one hear what are sometimes called, not too exactly, the truth of the mind and the truth of the heart and find them both one?

It is a major thesis of these chapters that this can happen only as we recognize that each speaks a different language; and that though each language can be understood, neither can be exhaustively translated into the other. In particular, we shall be thinking about the importance of myth, not only in the communication of faith, but also in our original apprehension of its meaning and truth.

CHAPTER TWO

IMAGES AND MYTHS

WE BEGAN this discussion by observing the mythological character of much in our confession as Christians and by noting the difficulty we are likely to feel in recognizing and acknowledging this fact. It was suggested that the basis of this inner resistance might be a very broad one—namely, an anomalous and altogether gratuitous suspicion that the concerns of faith and the concerns of truth are sometimes adverse to each other—and both the enormity and the tragic consequences of this illusion were exposed. It was indicated, however, that our objection might also be explained by a misunderstanding of what mythology is. It is with this misunderstanding—as well as with the true nature of the thing being misunderstood—that we shall now be concerned.

Undoubtedly the principal reason for our disposition to reject the idea of any association of mythology with our religious faith is our common presupposition that a myth is by definition untrue. The word suggests, perhaps most prominently, the fanciful and the fictitious; and in our ordinary speech when we speak of something as "mythical" we mean simply that it is nonexistent. Although it is not difficult to see how this has come to be the popular meaning of the term, its basic significance is, needless to say, quite different. The term really designates a kind of speech, a category of discourse, and is neutral as regards the question of truth. A myth can be false or true. One's judgment on this point, in the case of any particular myth, will be determined by the way one finds it meeting the criteria of truth which are appropriate to its category.

For just as speech is of many kinds, so the tests of truth are various. What is true, for example, in a historical drama will often not be true in a historical textbook. When Shaw in his *Saint Joan*[1] records a conversation in which a bishop of the Church and a feudal nobleman reflect on the significance of the emergence of nationalism and Protestantism in Europe, is the playwright telling the truth or not? Probably most of us reading or watching the play would say that he is. And yet we would know all the time that there is not the slightest reason to suppose that this conversation ever took place or even that these two particular individuals ever existed. But Shaw, we would say, is writing drama; and as drama this is true.

If we are making factual statements as, for example, about the speed of light or the date of an event, there is a definite set of criteria which our statements must fulfill. This is just as true when we make a logical or a mathematical statement

[1] Scene 4.

like, "The whole is greater than any of its parts"; but the criteria are not the same in this case as in the other. The two statements are in some ways incomparable; they belong to separate worlds of discourse, and the word "truth" has a somewhat different meaning in each. In the one kind of case, the statement is "true" if it corresponds with certain actual spatial or temporal conditions; in the other, if it possesses a certain inner consistency or coherence.

Now both of these kinds of speech are concerned with what are really abstractions—with bare facts or with concepts and their relations—and both can be carried on, or are supposed to be carried on, in precise, definable terms, terms which say exactly what is being thought. But most of our statements are of yet another kind. They deal with concretions. They have to do with what is immediately given in our actual experience, sensual, moral, and emotional. And if we go beyond the mere fact of the existence of such things and attempt to convey anything of their quality, their actual substance, their concrete reality—if we attempt this, we must perforce speak in terms largely drawn from our ways of sensing or feeling them. When we say, "The water is hot," we mean in most contexts or on most occasions, not that its temperature is above a certain fixed degree Fahrenheit, but that it "burns" our hands. So we may speak of the "refreshing" shade or of a "bracing" wind.

Such speech often, perhaps almost always, involves a transferring of terms from the area where they most properly belong to other areas; and we find ourselves employing metaphor or simile. The cold may be "bitter." Words of love may be "sweet." The coming of a friend may "warm" our hearts. It is clear that such terms do not apply to their objects in the same precise or matter-of-fact way as do the terms in the other cases. But who will say that they may not be, in their own equally legitimate way, quite as true? It was George Buttrick who told me of the man who observed that an error had obviously crept into the text of Shakespeare's lines about there being "books in the running brooks, sermons in stones."[2] Quite clearly, the man said, the lines were meant to read: "sermons in books, stones in running brooks." As between the two phrases, "sermons in books" and "sermons in stones," there can be no question which is the more interesting; but can it be said that either is more *true?* The simple and obvious fact is that each is true in its own very different but altogether appropriate way, and we become absurd when we apply to one category of statement the criteria of truth which we quite properly apply to the other.

Now it would be a mistake to suppose that in the case of the one kind of statement—the literal, factual kind—we mean to say something about objective reality, and our statement is "really" true because it corresponds with this reality, whereas in the more poetic kind of statement we are simply trying to express a subjective attitude or experience and the statement can be called true only in the sense that it succeeds in doing so. There is no doubt that the words "true" and "truth" are often, and quite properly, employed in this almost entirely subjective way. We speak of a "true" feeling, meaning a sincere feeling; and a form of words which expresses the feeling will also be "true." A work of art can be called "true" when it effectively embodies a real vision or mood of the artist, though its correspondence with any objective reality is remote indeed. Even in such a case, how-

[2] *As You Like It,* Act II, Scene 1.

ever, it would be rash to deny any kind of objective reference. When one calls such a work "true," does one not imply, at the very least, that the vision or mood is to some extent or at certain moments shared by others besides the artist and is therefore not entirely subjective? And does one not also probably imply that there is something in the real situation of man in the world which gives rise to, or answers to, the artist's feeling? If, hearing Horatio in *Hamlet* say,

> But, look, the morn, in russet mantle clad,
> Walks o'er the dew of yon high eastward hill,[3]

we find his words "true," we mean that we too have seen the dawn thus "walk" and that, moreover, it does in fact thus "walk." Such a statement could not be called "true" if some such objective reference were not found in it.

In other words, when we say there are "books in the running brooks," we are making a statement which, if we regard it as true at all, is for us objectively true—quite as much so as the statement that stones are there. We mean that "running brooks" have something to teach us—that they *really* do. So also if one reads a scene in a play and thinks of it as true, one means that such and such people in such and such a situation would really act, or at least might be expected to act, in just this way. If the scene happens to be a representation of some actual event or development, it may have objective truth of a more specific kind and indeed is not as fully true as it might be if it does not. I referred earlier to a scene in Shaw's *Saint Joan* involving a bishop and a nobleman. That scene could be called true if it is psychologically true—that is, if, given the situation which has developed in

[3] Act I, Scene 1.

the play, the churchman and the feudal lord, as their characters have emerged, might plausibly have spoken to each other in the indicated way. But would we regard the scene as being fully true if it were not seen as being also historically true? And by applying that phrase one will mean, not that the scene actually took place, but—something equally objective—that what has proved to be the real significance of the events surrounding the career of Joan of Arc is set forth in the dramatist's quite imaginary picture.

Images, then (we are saying generally), can be true—that is, they can express actual qualities of actual things as known in experience or as carried in memory. Their truth can be as "objective" as that of mathematical or logical statements or of statements of scientific fact. All statements of the latter kind are concerned with abstractions—with the quantities or the quantitative relations of things—but objects in their concrete reality have *qualities*, and these qualities can be expressed and communicated only through images. B. H. Streeter illuminates the point by putting side by side a map of Venice and one of Turner's paintings of that city.[4] Who would dream of denying that the painting can be just as certainly true—objectively true—as even the most accurate map?

One difference as regards the truth of the two kinds of representation is at once apparent and will be seen as particularly important and relevant when we turn, in a moment, from images in general to myths in particular. There can be only one "true" map of Venice, but there may be many "true" paintings. The measurable dimensions and relations of an object can be truly stated in only one way; but its qual-

[4] *Reality* (London: Macmillan and Company, 1926), pp. 31ff.

ity—its reality as felt or experienced—not only is this inexhaustible, having innumerable faces or aspects, but we recognize also that even a single aspect can be variously, but still quite truly, expressed. The "morn" does not always present itself in "russet" hue; and even when it does, Shakespeare's line is not the only way it can be truly spoken of. Shakespeare himself has used other images, equally appropriate and true; and many other metaphors in many other poets may come to mind. However apt, or apparently perfect, a metaphor may be, it is always conceivable that an even apter one, or at least another just as apt, could be found. So there may be a dozen very different, but equally true, portraits of the same person. And to say that Shaw's *Joan* is true does not mean saying that another dramatist's very different play on the same theme may not also be true. In other words, while we shall always need figures or pictures of some kind if we would express the concrete reality of something in our experience, we are not limited to any one figure or picture. Although the use of images is unavoidable, no particular image is indispensable. We are always aware of the distinction between the reality known in our experience and our ways of speaking about it, and we are thus in no danger of mistaking the figurative or allusive character of our speech.

It is precisely this distinction which in mythology is obscured or drops from sight. And here is to be seen, perhaps, the most significant mark of the myth as compared with what we ordinarily call "figures of speech." The myth claims a kind of relation to objective, factual truth which other forms of allusive discourse do not claim. We become aware of this difference when we observe the tendency of the myth to be exclusive or definitive. We have just been noting how there can be a quite indefinite proliferation of metaphors or similes in reference to the same object; there cannot be of myths. This limitation is partly owing to the fact that, whereas similes and metaphors, not to say works of art like plays or paintings, are the creations of individuals, myths are folk creations. The true myth is never consciously invented; it is a cultural inheritance. Indeed, a myth may have been so long and intimately associated with the distinctive life of a particular religious community that it is now a kind of indispensable symbol of its concrete reality, an actual carrier of its vitality and power. A new generation may reinterpret such a myth—indeed often it must—but it cannot conceivably substitute another myth for it.

Important as this consideration is, however, another peculiarity of the myth is even more important in this connection. This is its claim, not only to express and describe the felt reality, or quality, of an object, but also to account for it, to explain its origin. There may be many ways of truly describing a reality, but, one is likely to feel, there can hardly be many ways of truly explaining it.

When the modern poet speaks of the morn as "walking o'er the dew . . . ," he is making use of a conscious metaphor and knows quite well that he might equally truly speak of the morn in other ways. But when the ancient poet, responding in the same imaginative way to the glory in the east, identifies the "russet" figure as Aurora rising from the sea and with rosy fingers dropping dew on the earth, we have a myth. For the ancient poet thinks of himself, not only as *describing* the morn, but also, and chiefly, as *explaining* its coming. The situation is not that the dawn is being thought of as like the moving figure or as suggesting the moving figure; the dawn *is* the moving figure.

To be sure, we may easily exaggerate the realism or matter-of-fact-ness with which the ancient understood his myths. I think it is fair to assume that he did not take them as being literally true, in our sense of that phrase. But this would not usually have been because he thought of them as being *not* literally true, but rather because he was far less sharply aware than we of the distinction between the kinds of truth we have been discussing. What we call the literal and what we call the figurative or symbolical could flow together for him to an extent they cannot for us. What for us must have the character of a figure of speech could for him be also a more direct and factual account of reality. The pictures of Proteus and Triton which Wordsworth evokes in his familiar sonnet can have for us the kind of truth a good metaphor or simile can have. But for the ancient they had, in addition, another kind of truth: Proteus rose, in very fact, "from the sea," and "old Triton" really blew "his wreathèd horn." What is for us a suggestion or hint of the felt quality of an experienced reality could be for him a quite objective and definitive explanation of it as well. The stories of the gods were for him not only effective dramatic representations of real aspects of man's world; they also told him how the world under its various aspects came to be. In a word, images which for us are metaphor were for him myth.

The assertion that belief in the objective truth of the myth is essential to its being truly a myth—this assertion is not incompatible with the emphasis among contemporary anthropologists and historians of religion upon what is called its "archetypal and paradigmatic" character. This phrase is taken from one of the most brilliant of these, Mircea Eliade, who argues eloquently, and with great learning, that for primitive man what was actual in time and place had reality only because it participated, through repetition or imitation, in certain original acts of gods or divine heroes. Thus each New Year was a fresh creation of the world, and the same primordial creative deed was seen as reenacted in such events as conception and birth and in ceremonial cleansings and renewals. Eliade's principal point is that archaic man in this way "annuls time"; he is able to live "in a continual present" and thus escape from the intolerable pressures of historical existence.[5] To the latter point we shall need to return later, when we discuss, with special reference to the Hebrew-Christian tradition, the relation of myth to history. At the moment I am interested only in saying that this stress upon the "paradigmatic" nature of the god's actions as told in the myths, far from requiring a devaluation of their objective truth, rather enhances it. For according to this understanding, not only were the myths true; they alone were really true. The repetitive events which make up our actual experience have reality at all only because they share in the ultimate reality of the original events.

To be sure, these original events may have been thought of as taking place, not in *our* time, but in what Eliade calls "mythical time"; but, even so, they did take place, and only because they did can anything else real or authentic be said to exist. This objective truth of myth and its explanatory function are emphasized by Eliade when he writes:

[5] *Cosmos and History*, tr. Willard R. Trask (New York: Harper and Brothers, 1959).

Myth narrates a sacred history; it relates an event which took place in primordial Time, the fabled time of the "beginnings." In other words, myth tells how, through the deeds of Supernatural Beings, a reality came into existence, be it the whole of reality, the Cosmos, or only a fragment of reality—an island, a species of plant, a particular kind of human behavior, an institution. Myth, then, is always an account of a "creation"; it relates how something was produced, began to *be*.[6]

Thus the mythological has a curious, almost paradoxical, double character. On the one hand, the myth is an imaginative and in a measure fanciful story; it must be such, for it is by definition an account of a divine action, and no human narrative of a divine action could conceivably be literally true. Whatever God "does," the words which designate or describe our own actions cannot in the same way designate or describe his. On the other hand, however, a myth is not a myth if the action of God which it describes in its own poetic fashion is not believed actually to have taken place. "Myth," writes Henri Frankfort, "is a form of poetry which transcends poetry in that it proclaims a truth."[7] If I understand Paul Tillich correctly, his words are pertinent: "Only when one's thinking has objective reference can a truly mythical element pulsate through it."[8] A myth is not an authentic myth if it is not believed.

If what I have been saying points, or comes anywhere

[6] *Myth and Reality* (New York: Harper and Row, 1963), pp. 5–6.

[7] "Myth and Reality," in H. and H. A. Frankfort, *The Intellectual Character of Ancient Man* (Chicago: University of Chicago Press, 1946), p. 8.

[8] "The Religious Symbol," *Daedalus*, Summer, 1958, p. 21; see also p. 18–20.

near to pointing, to an important difference between the figurative in general and the mythological in particular, the question may be asked whether the mythological has any legitimate, or in the long run possible, place in the modern world. Must not all the ancient myths have for us the character of metaphor or something like it? We may preserve them as part of a cultural tradition, but can they be for us "myths" any longer? Are they not mere figures of speech, true only in the way certain works of art are true—that is, suggesting by the use of images true dimensions of man's existence and effectively expressing the quality of something in his experience, but without what we should ordinarily call objective truth, whether factual or metaphysical? We can value them; but we cannot believe them.

To take this position would obviously be to deny the continuing possibility of the mythological in any real sense of the term. But it would also be to deny the possibility of religion. It would mean the reduction of religion to aestheticism—or, if one objects to the term "reduction," the identification of the one with the other. Actually, however, not only are the two distinguishable, but religion is by far the deeper, and more creative, element in man's nature and in his response to the world. The Proteus and Triton of poetry are later than, derived from, and would be impossible without, the Proteus and Triton of religion. When Edna St. Vincent Millay in an ecstatic contemplation of a New England wood in autumn exclaimed,

Lord, I do fear
Thou'st made the world too beautiful this year,[9]

[9] From *Collected Poems*, Harper & Row. Copyright 1913, 1940 by Edna St. Vincent Millay, by permission of Norma Millay Ellis.

she may have been expressing a merely temporary mood and making a purely aesthetic response to her immediate environment. But the words came to her only because an earlier generation were expressing what they knew to be the actual explanation of the glory of the world when they sang: "In his hands are all the corners of the earth; and the strength of the hills is his also. The sea is his and he made it and his hands prepared the dry land." And her words have vitality and power only because, in our own generation, we deeply "remember," if nothing more, that this is really true. The aesthetic power of the myth depends upon its continuing to have this kind of objective truth.

But how, we are asking, can this be? How can modern religious man both have myths (as he must to be religious) and at the same time know that it is myths he has (as he must if he is modern)? How can myths have reality as myths— that is, how can they have the kind of value a myth must have to be a myth—once we recognize them as myths? There is no doubt that they can have this reality and this value—the existence of vital religion in the modern world testifies as much—but how is this to be explained? How can this be? We must look further and more closely at what it means for a myth to be true. How does one believe a myth?

The clue to the answer lies, I believe, in the distinction between the two elements in the intention of myth which we have noted—namely, its intention to convey the quality of some reality in our experience and its intention to account for the origin of this reality as objective fact. I have said that in the ancient mythology the two intentions were not distinguished clearly, if at all. Aurora's "rosy fingers" served both to suggest the mystery and beauty of the dawn and to designate the cause or source (or, if you will, the archetype) of it. For the modern religious person, however, the two elements must be clearly distinguished. One must recognize in any particular myth or story the presence of what I shall call for convenience the "existential-expressive" and the "objective-explanatory." Not that the two can be separated; if we accept the myth, we shall accept it as a whole. Still, we shall not be accepting each element in the same way. We shall accept the myth as "expressive" if it seems to us to convey in the only possible or adequate way the felt reality, the concrete meaning, of something in our existence; we shall accept it as "explanatory" if we find ourselves accounting for this "something" by the actual objective act of God of which the myth intends to speak. We do not find the myth true unless we find it true in both senses, although the meaning of the word "true" in the two cases will not be the same.

Perhaps so far as the Christian tradition is concerned, the distinction between the two elements can most clearly be seen in the area of eschatological mythology. We are bound to recognize the figurative, the highly imaginative, character of the language in which the Church has expressed its hopes for the ultimate future. The rich diversity of the images it has used—not to speak of their obvious incompatibility with one another if taken with any literalness—makes this character particularly clear. Moreover, it is manifest that, in this area especially, the only alternative to such imaginative speech is silence. Either we speak of our dead as "in Abraham's bosom," as "being with Christ," as "asleep in Christ" awaiting the "general resurrection" and the Lord's "return," or in some similar way; or else we refrain from speaking. But this last we cannot do; our hopes are real and they clamor for expression. We *must* say that God will save us from death, that he will redeem our life from destruction, that by his mercy our partial, broken selves shall be made whole, that we shall see God. We actually expect this in our own future; we are convinced that it belongs to the future, or to the already realized present, of our dead. In other words, there is an objective or factual element in this mythology; and it would not be true mythology if this were not the case. To be sure, we cannot speak of what God will do for us "in the last day" without using language which belongs almost entirely to the imagination, but this does not mean that we are doubting the actuality of his doing it.

This is just as true of the opening story in the biblical mythology as of the final one. What does it mean to accept the biblical myth of the creation and fall of man? It means, first of all, I should say, accepting what is clearly seen to be an imaginative story as truly "expressive" of man's existential condition. Looked at so, the narrative in the first two chapters of Genesis is not an account of some actual happenings which, if we were well enough informed, might be given dates in time and located precisely in earthly or stellar space. Rather, it is a way of expressing what man is. If one sees man in Rousseauistic fashion as simply good or if one takes the opposite, the purely cynical, view, in neither case can this myth seem true. But if one sees man, oneself and mankind as a whole, as basically good and sound but, as it were, maimed or marred, then one will feel both the appeal and the essential truth of this ancient story. Human nature, it will seem to such a one, is a divine thing strangely twisted or distorted. Capable of, and in a measure actually knowing, a freedom which nothing else in nature can know, man has fallen into a slavery more abject and degrading than anything the determinism of nature can produce.

This existential understanding of man's actual nature has never been voiced more eloquently than by Paul: "I do not do the good I want, but the evil I do not want is what I do. . . . I delight in the law of God, in my inmost self, but I see in my members another law at war with the law of my mind and making me captive to the law of sin which dwells in my members. Wretched man that I am! Who will deliver me from this body of death?"[10] However different our own psychological terminology might be, can we fail to understand what Paul is saying here? Do we not know the same conflict, the same inner contradiction in ourselves? And do we not see it written large in every form of our corporate existence? If so, we shall not reject the story that God crowned his creation of all things by making man in his own likeness and for companionship with himself, but only to see this son of his love, denying his creaturehood and rebelling against his Creator, fall into bondage to demonic powers of evil. This is not the only biblical story in which this understanding is expressed. One thinks, for example, of the images of the sheep lost from the fold where it belongs, and therefore utterly helpless and distraught, and of the son estranged and separated from his true home, and therefore wretched in his slavery and hunger.

The Genesis story, however, is not a parable, as these are; it is a myth. Accepting it, therefore, means more than seeing it as an apt metaphor or simile or as an instructive fable. One

---

[10] Rom. 7: 19, 22–24. Biblical quotations, here and elsewhere in this book, are generally from the Revised Standard Version.

will see it, not only as truly "expressive" of our existential condition, but also as truly "explanatory" in a more objective sense. It does not say, "It is as though this happened"; it says, "This happened." To find it true means finding that it carries at its heart an objective or factual truth which can be expressed in no other way. One who accepts it will be affirming that back of or underneath—yes, and in some real sense prior to—the whole cosmic order and our own existence as men is God's reality; that God's goodness is the creative and constitutive principle in the actual world; and that evil, however its ultimate origins are to be explained and whether it is associated more closely with man's finitude or with his freedom, is essentially alien, involves man in a betrayal and denial of his true nature, and must finally be overcome.

This understanding, simply as abstract idea, might perhaps be stated in nonmythological terms, although I confess that I do not see clearly how this could be. What does seem clear to me, however, is that the concrete content of that understanding, the quality or "feel" of it, the particular way of realizing it which belongs to the historical life of Israel and later of the Church, cannot be otherwise designated or expressed. The story of man's creation and fall is as ancient as the cultural community itself and is the product of the same historical process. So long as we belong to that community and find the roots of our spiritual life in that tradition, so long shall we, not only remember this story, but also deeply believe it.

CHAPTER THREE

OUR NEED OF MYTHS

Thus far the word "myth" has been used without any attempt to define it, and I hope I shall be forgiven if I continue to avoid formal definition. The term has a variety of uses in a variety of connections and, as we have several times had occasion to observe, is notoriously difficult to define. Since our discussion does not presume to consider mythology in its whole range, but only in a single connection, a comprehensive definition is perhaps not required. It is important, however, that I make as clear as possible what I conceive to be the meaning of the word in connection with the biblical and credal materials we are considering, and I can hardly postpone longer some attempt at formulating in more concise and coherent fashion what has thus far emerged only in partial statements or by implication. I shall try to say, then, what (for the most part at any rate) I have meant by the term and what I shall more consistently mean by it as this discussion proceeds.

Even this is by no means easy. Perhaps the following "notes" will suffice: (1) By "myth" I mean a story—that is, an imaginative narrative—dealing with a cosmically significant act of God (or of some superhuman being). By "cosmically significant act" is meant an act of decisive importance for the world, particularly the world of men, whose response to it may be an essential part of the story. This action may be represented as taking place in a prehistorical, a historical, or a posthistorical epoch; but it is a particular action at a particular time. (2) This narrative will have had its source in the common life of a human community, will bear the marks of its culture, and will persist over the generations as a part of its tradition. (3) The community will prize the story because it suggests, or answers to, and is believed actually to explain or account for, something distinctive and important in human existence, and particularly in its own. (4) Because of the relation in which the story thus stands to the actual existence of the community, it will have become itself an inseparable and indispensable part of the community's life and, for those sharing that life, an irreplaceable symbol, an actual carrier of its power.

A myth, I should say, is truly a myth—and, to participants in the culture to which it belongs, will seem, by the same token, to be a *true* myth—when these four conditions apply.

All of these "notes" have been implied in what has already been said, although some of them are now stated in a way to anticipate our later discussion. Each one, it will be observed, has, in addition to its positive significance, a certain exclusive force. When we define the "myth" as a narrative, we exclude anything merely descriptive or expository, no matter how allusive or figurative its language may be. (A descriptive or expository passage may make use of terms derived from, or reminiscent of, a myth and may therefore be in a certain sense "mythological"; but it is not a myth. A myth is a story.) When we specify as a myth's principal subject matter an "act of God"—and a "cosmically significant act" at that—we separate the myth from the innumerable legends or tales in every cultural tradition which are concerned primarily with human heroes and their deeds. To locate the origins of myth in the life of a religious community is to deny the possibility of conscious or intentional invention. Myths are social, not individual, creations. Finally, to limit the myth to what has become "irreplaceable symbol" of something distinctive and important in the community's existence is to reserve the term for a relatively small number of stories. Not every miracle story deserves to be called a "myth." Only the indispensable story is worthy of the name.

This last stipulation may seem particularly questionable. Is it not arbitrary thus to limit the term? Who is to separate out the indispensable stories in a community's traditions? Is it not likely that what will seem dispensable to one individual or group, or to one age or generation, will seem irreplaceable to another? These are good questions and some consideration must be given them.

At the outset we should recognize that a measure of what may be called "subjectivism" cannot be excluded from the very definition of myth. I have ventured to say that a myth is truly a myth only if it is believed. This means that a particular myth is not a myth *for me* if I do not find it true; and if, not finding it true, I refer to it as a myth at all, it can be only because I know others do. We can speak of the myths of the ancient Greeks or Persians only because, although we do not believe them, we know they did. When it happens that a myth is no longer believed within some community or culture, it has ceased to be a myth. It may have had that character at an earlier time, but it has it no longer. It may still have value in suggesting or recalling the real quality of something in human experience, but, as we have seen, although this is enough to make a good metaphor, or a good work of art, it is not enough to make a good myth. It will be seen, then, that in making the questionable stipulation I am speaking from the point of view of a believer, who alone can have direct and immediate knowledge of the myth as myth. I am speaking as from within the community to which the myth belongs. I am saying that *from this point of view* a myth must be indispensable if it is to be believed—that is, if it is to be truly a myth at all.

This condition has always, I should say, applied in some measure, but it has become especially important and pertinent in the modern period. It will be recalled that in the preceding chapter I called attention to the fact that although figures of speech can have almost endless variety, even when the same object is being described, myths always tend to be exclusive. They presume to say, not what things are *like* (they might be like any number of things), but what they actually are and how they came to be. It is to be assumed, for example, that in Greece for some group at some time, to refer to Eos (Aurora) was the only adequate way of referring to the dawn, and that, in the same group or another, one could not speak definitively of the sun without speaking of

Helios. But with the rise of ancient science and philosophy and the progressive extension of their attitude and method, one after another of the ancient myths became dispensable. One might still find Aurora a useful image in referring to or describing the dawn; but eventually no one any longer needed Aurora to account for its coming. And because she was no longer indispensable to the designating and explicating of something in men's existence or in the existence of the world as they experienced it, she was no longer really credible. But if the myths were already under such pressure, even in the ancient world, what shall we say of their chances of survival in the modern period? In a word, the ancient religious myths have for a long time been on the defensive, and in the contemporary age only the absolutely indispensable myth can hope to survive. One can believe only the myths one has to believe.

This association of truth with necessity is not at all peculiar to myth. It is a universally valid principle in the intellectual life. We speak of truth as setting us free; but it does so, paradoxically enough, by making an absolute claim on us. There is something coercive about truth, wherever it is found and however it is expressed. One is no more free to accept truth than to reject it. One has no right to regard as true what one is not forced to regard as true. The only justification for agreeing to a logical or mathematical conclusion is that one finds one has to. Even in areas of our knowledge (as in history and geography) where absolutely certain truth is not attainable, but only reasonably probable truth—even here the principle still holds: one is justified in regarding as "probably true" only what one is required to regard as "probably true." If our intellectual activity were always carried on with complete integrity, we should never be able to believe what we were not inwardly constrained to believe.

William James in an influential essay of a generation ago celebrated what he called "the will to believe."[1] The argument was that where a matter of fact is uncertain and must in the nature of the case remain uncertain (that is, neither its truth nor its falseness can be demonstrated), but is at the same time of such a kind that the whole meaning of our existence is dependent on its being true—in such a case, one must, in effect, decide whether it is true or not. One cannot leave the question open; one must commit oneself one way or the other. And, it was concluded, since one must, in effect, either affirm or deny, one is justified in affirming. But is there not a *non sequitur* in the argument? It is true that I may have to commit myself *in action* when I am really uncertain of the vitally relevant facts—actually we find ourselves doing this constantly in decisions on matters great and small—but I see no way in which, by an act of will, I can change uncertainty to certainty or affirm as true what I am not inwardly required to acknowledge as true.

It should not seem strange, then, to say that only necessary myths can seem true, and this ought especially to be the case in a time like our own when the very possibility of a true myth has been brought under such constant and vigorous challenge. Whatever the situation in the past, an ancient religious myth must, in the modern world, seem clearly indispensable if it is to be credible and, therefore, if it is to continue to exist as a myth at all.

[1] *The Will to Believe and Other Essays in Popular Philosophy* (New York and London: Longmans Green and Company, 1897).

By "indispensable" I mean essential to our designating and expressing, and even to our grasping, or being grasped by, some reality in our own existence. The religious certainties to which true myths answer are, as we have often noted, existential certainties. They are not mere facts about the external world in time and space. They are not abstract or rational truths. They are neither deductions from premises nor inductions from data. They are not susceptible of being proved. But the reason they cannot be demonstrated is not that these realities are not sure enough, but rather that they are too sure. They cannot be proved for the same reason an axiom cannot be proved: no datum can be found as a *basis* of proof which is not less certain than the proposed *object* of proof. No premises can be as sure as the conclusion already is. God's reality cannot be established by any argument, but only because we already know it in the depths of our own existence. We know it whether we know that we know it or not. As we have been reminded before, we experience it as Emptiness or Nothingness if in no other way. We may know only an ultimate, unassuageable Hunger or Loneliness. But it is God we know in this Void—and indeed we must continue to know him so if we are to know him in any other way, as well. Religious experience is "deep calling unto deep"; and we cannot separate one "deep" from the other—the "deep" of our need of God and the "deep" of the God we need. God makes himself known as both Void and Fullness, as both Question and Answer, and does so in the depths of our own life.

In a word, the being of God and the relation in which he stands to us are not so-called objective facts to be established by arguments, nor are they mere hypotheses on the truth of which we are to venture our lives. They are involved in our being as the men we are and, once recognized, can as little be doubted as we can doubt our own inner existence. Such existential realities cannot, except in the most superficial and partial way, be expressed in abstract conceptual terms. It is not only true that one cannot speak of them except with concrete images; one cannot grasp them otherwise oneself. The terms we have just been using—Void, Hunger, Loneliness, as well as such words as Judge, Companion, Father—belong inevitably to our way of speaking of God because they belong inseparably to our way of knowing him.

This general fact about the nature of what we are calling "existential realities" and about the kind of terms in which they must be expressed is not, however, a sufficient explanation of why some particular myth or story is essential and irreplaceable. We need to recognize a further fact, also "existential"; the existence in which these "realities" are found is not an individualistic thing. No man exists—in any sense of that word—apart from others. One's own unique existence is really one's own unique way of participating in certain corporate existences created in nature and history. Sometimes we distinguish between men as men and as members of various cultural groups. For most practical purposes in discussion this is unexceptionable; but actually the distinction is not as clear as it may seem. Is there such a thing as "men as men"? Must we not say that a purely human—in the sense of a merely or barely human, a generalized human—existence would be an abstraction and not an existence at all?

The Church has its own distinctive existence, and the Christian is such in virtue of his sharing in it. This existence had a historical beginning, and the Church's essential nature

—its own unique inner being—was determined in the moment of its birth. But it is also true that in that same moment were created the dramatic forms for the expressing of this reality; and the forms, simply on that account, are inseparable from it. One could not abandon the ancient images and substitute modern images for them without losing contact with the concrete historical reality itself. When we say, then, that a Christian myth is indispensable, we are saying that something of decisive importance in the inner being and nature of the Church cannot be expressed or explained or even definitively referred to, except in terms of it. Such a myth is thus an irreplaceable symbol.[2]

I said earlier that not every miracle story deserves to be called a "myth," and the point I have just been trying to make may be clarified if we take an example. Consider the story of the raising of Lazarus from the dead as recorded in the eleventh chapter of the Gospel of John. Jesus, having heard that his friend Lazarus was ill, arrives at his home only after he has been dead four days. Jesus finds Mary, Lazarus' sister, and many of her friends overwhelmed with grief and despair; but Martha, another sister, is sufficiently alert to the

[2] Paul Tillich is using the word "symbol" rather than "myth," but since I am now discussing myth (and for our purposes have defined it) as "irreplaceable symbol," his words apply: "The sign is interchangeable at will. It does not arise from necessity, for it has no inner power. The symbol, however, does possess a necessary character. It cannot be exchanged. It can only disappear when, through dissolution, it loses its inner power. Nor can it be merely constructed; it can only be created. Words and signs originally had a symbolic character. They conveyed the meaning which they expressed with an inherent power of their own. In the course of evolution and as a result of the transition from the mystical to the technical view of the world, they have lost their symbolic character, though not entirely. Once having lost their innate power they became

possible significance of Jesus' presence for him to be able to say to her with some hope of her understanding: "I am the resurrection and the life; he who believes in me, though he die, yet shall he live, and whoever lives and believes in me shall never die." He asks Martha if she believes this, and she tells him that she does. Later Jesus went to the tomb, ordered that the stone be moved from the door, reminded Martha and others that through the Father's favor to him they were about to witness the "glory of God," and then "cried with a loud voice, 'Lazarus, come out.' The dead man came out, his hands and feet bound with bandages, and his face wrapped with a cloth. Jesus said to them, 'Unbind him, and let him go.' "

No more striking miracle story could be cited, perhaps. But, although most of us would probably regard it, in whole or part, as a creation of the imagination, it is not a myth. To be sure, it is like a myth in being the story of a deed of God, for Christ in the Fourth Gospel is virtually a divine being (although the story could also easily be thought of as concerned with the actions of a divinely endowed man, in which case it would be more truly a legend than a myth). It is also, and more unquestionably, like a myth in having its origin in the experience of the community and in answering

---

signs. The pictorial symbols of religious art were originally charged with a magical power, with the loss of which they became a conventional sign-language and almost forfeited their genuine symbolic character" ("The Religious Symbol," *Daedalus*, Summer, 1958, p. 4). See also on this power of the symbol, the moving words of Karl Jaspers, *Truth and Symbol*, tr. Jean T. Wilde, William Kluback, and William Kimmel (New Haven: College and University Press, 1959), pp. 37–64. A. N. Wilder's book *The Language of the Gospel* (New York: Harper and Row, 1964), which appeared after my manuscript was in the publisher's hands, is relevant and useful here as at many other points in our argument; see esp. its final chapter "Image, Symbol, Myth."

to the realities in its existence—that is, to the new life of faith, devotion, and hope which the early Church knew. But though the story may wonderfully illustrate this new life, it cannot be thought of, and has never been thought of, as actually accounting for it. No one has claimed, or would claim, that if this incident had not happened, the new life would not have come to be. Nor would anyone argue that the world would be essentially different from what it is or that mankind would be related to God in any significantly different way, if Lazarus had not been raised. In other words, I do not need this story to express or to explain anything in my existence as a Christian. Nothing in my experience forces me to accept this story as an actual occurrence. It is thus not indispensable and, therefore, for this reason, if for no other, lacks the status of a myth.

In contrast, consider the story—the great story, of which the Lazarus story and every other miracle story in the Gospels is, as it were, a kind of pale echo—the story of how God so loved the world which had become estranged from him that at a particular time long ago he sent into it his Son to redeem it, whom in our rebellious and ruthless pride we slew. But God's love, the story goes on to say, did not forsake us but turned the very death of the Anointed One into a means of our salvation, raising him from the grave and offering us peace and life as sharers in a new creation, the body of his resurrection, the Church in heaven and on earth.

Here we have a *myth* in that entirely appreciatory sense which that term has in this discussion. Would we not say that it is the only distinctively Christian myth? Certainly, it is the basic one, of which all others are variations or from which they are derived. This story does not merely illustrate or exemplify, as a good allegory or simile might and as the

miracle stories often do, something distinctive in the quality
of the community's existence; this story entirely and definitively expresses and explains it. The Christian may be fully
aware of the imaginative character of the story's terms. If
he is at all thoughtful, he will know that he is using human
images when he speaks of God's having a "Son," or of his
"sending" him, or of the death of Christ as a means of expia-
tion, or of God's exalting Jesus from the tomb to a seat on his
own right hand—images which in the nature of the case cannot apply. He will know, in other words, that he is dealing
with a "story." But it is bound to be for him a true story—
true, not only because it alone adequately expresses the felt
reality of his existence as a Christian, but true also because
he knows that what the story is trying to describe actually
occurred. He believes, and is bound by his very existence as
a Christian to believe, that in Jesus and the event which happened around him the God of heaven and earth (without
ceasing to be such: hence the references to the "Son" or the
"Word") did in very fact enter human history, did in very
fact identify himself with man in a complete and absolutely
unprecedented way, and did all of this in order to overcome
our hostility and in very fact to "reconcile the world unto
himself."[3] The story is thus an indispensable statement and
an irreplaceable symbol of the inner existence of the Church.

If the essential thing the Christian believes is that God
"acted" in Christ ("Christ" meaning "Jesus and the event
which happened around him") to bring about this reconcili-

[3] It is in line with the argument of this book to observe that when I
began this sentence I intended to make a nonmythological statement and
that I have ended with another mythological one. One cannot make a nonmythological statement on this theme.

ation and if he recognizes the necessarily highly figurative, the nonliteral, character of any account of the content of this "action," can it be said that he believes a *myth?* This question, or one very much like it, has figured prominently in the discussions which have been going on in Germany for more than a decade over what has come to be called "demythologizing." The great German New Testament scholar and theologian, Rudolf Bultmann, initiated them with an essay which urged both the necessity of the Church's getting free from the mythology in terms of which its faith was first expressed and also the possibility of its doing so through a utilization of categories of contemporary existentialist thought. According to the demythologizers, the ancient Christian myths are to be taken as modes of human "self-understanding," embodying realities and possibilities of authentic and universal human existence, and may be fully and exhaustively translated into these existentialist terms. Bultmann, however, also believes profoundly in the decisive significance for human life—the "once-for-all-ness"—of the event which happened around Jesus and finds it both possible and necessary to affirm that God "acted" in this event. The proclamation of this action is called by him the "kerygma" (the Greek word for the announcement of an event). "Kerygma" and "myth" must, according to Bultmann, be clearly distinguished from each other and can to a degree be separated. The myths must be demythologized; the kerygma stands intact.[4]

    [4] The best introduction to this discussion for the English-speaking reader is provided by the two volumes of *Kerygma and Myth* (London: Society for the Promotion of Christian Knowledge, 1954 and 1962), both edited (in the original German edition) by Hans Werner Bartsch and

Although it is very easy to oversimplify the issues in the long and widespread controversy, involving both theologians and philosophers, which has followed upon Bultmann's essay, it may not be too wide of the mark to say that the argument has largely turned on the question whether this distinction between myth and kerygma is possible. Generally speaking, all of Bultmann's opponents agree with one another that it is not. They insist that we cannot separate the proclamation that God acted in Christ from the story of what that action was. If the story is mythological and subject to demythologization (that is, to exhaustive interpretation as descriptive of present existence), then the same must be said of the kerygma. For this reason orthodox Christian critics tend to resist demythologization; they see the implied admission of the need of it as placing in jeopardy the actuality of God's once-for-all action in Christ. The more liberal Christian, as well as the secular, critics not only welcome it, but object that Bultmann does not carry it far enough. The "orthodox," in other words, are inclined to see what Bult-

---

translated into English by Reginald H. Fuller. These books contain a number of essays by Bultmann as well as by others. See also Bultmann's own *Jesus Christ and Mythology* (New York: Charles Scribner's Sons, 1958). Important critical comment on the issues of the German controversy may be found in Ian Henderson, *Myth in the New Testament* (London: Student Christian Movement Press, 1952); G. V. Jones, *Christology and Myth in the New Testament* (London: George Allen and Unwin, 1956); B. Throckmorton, *The New Testament and Mythology* (Philadelphia: Westminster Press, 1959); John Macquarrie, *The Scope of Demythologizing* (New York: Harper and Brothers, 1960); Schubert M. Ogden, *Christ without Myth* (New York: Harper and Brothers, 1961); and in many other books. Of those named I have found Professor Macquarrie's most helpful. See also the admirable brief review by A. N. Wilder, "Mythology and the New Testament," *Journal of Biblical Literature*, LXIX (1950), 113ff.

mann calls myth as belonging essentially to the kerygma and therefore as being true in the same way the kerygma is true; the more "radical," to see the kerygma as belonging essentially to myth and therefore as being false—false, that is, except as an ancient way of referring to realities and possibilities of human existence.

What shall we say about these issues? I hope we shall be ready to agree with Bultmann on the importance of the Church's recognizing the mythological character of much in the New Testament and in the Creeds. We should also be prepared to agree with him in seeing a distinction of importance between the affirmation, on the one hand, that God was in very fact acting in the event and, on the other, the story of the descent, the sacrifice or struggle, and the final exaltation of the Christ, in terms of which that affirmation is made. But what is the relation between the two elements? Can they be separated? Can the affirmation be made if the story is not told?

On this point, I am not sure I understand Bultmann and shall not venture to interpret him. For myself, however, I should want to say something like this: What Bultmann means by the "kerygma" seems to me to correspond roughly with what I have ventured to call the "objective-explanatory" in the intention of the myth. The kerygma answers to, in the sense of seeking to account for, the distinctive life of the Church. It is the affirmation that it was God who brought this community into being and that he did so in the event which centered in Jesus of Nazareth. (The "once-for-all-ness" of the event is only another way of referring to the distinctive identity, the historical uniqueness, of the Church.) But it would not suffice to say this so barely. So merely "factual" a statement would not express anything of the rich, concrete fullness, the realized quality, of the community's life of love, faith, and hope or convey any of the concrete meaning of Christ himself, both remembered and present, which is the very breath of the Church's existence. This quality and meaning are embodied in the story; and because they can be designated and expressed in no other way, the story is inseparable from the kerygma and shares in its truth. But it is not less truly myth on that account. For it is the essential nature of myth to affirm as actual fact an occurrence whose concrete content cannot be literally expressed or, to put it in the obverse way, to describe in imaginative terms an occurrence which, nevertheless, is confidently affirmed to have taken place. I can see no way of breaking up this unity.

As for "demythologization," if by this term we mean doing our best to interpret the myth (as Bultmann says he does), there can be no doubt of its legitimacy, and indeed of its necessity. By this "interpreting" we shall mean, not translating the myth into adequate conceptual or matter-of-fact terms, but rather (again with Bultmann, as I understand him) recognizing and identifying the character, or possibility, of our actual existence to which it points and of which it is the symbol. But one further thing needs to be said—and here one might wish that Bultmann spoke more clearly—namely, that the "existence" of which the christological myths are an expression is the *Church's* existence; the reality they designate is not an individual thing but is the distinctive inner being of a particular historical community. Because these stories were created in the same historical moment as the Church itself, they belong integrally and inalienably to the community; they both answer to and evoke the depths of its own peculiar life; they share in its vitality and power. Truly to interpret them is to see them as pointing, not to universal human existence only, but to the particular existence of the Church. It is this fact which, above all others, constitutes the indispensability of the myth.

CHAPTER FOUR

MYTH AND HISTORY

O UR principal concern with myth has been with its truth —with whether myths *can* be true, with *how* or in what sense they may be true, and with *when* or under what conditions a particular myth is in fact true. All of these matters have been considered only in a very general and summary way. But the christological myth, which came particularly into view toward the end of the preceding chapter, involves a more specific question which we have so far hardly touched on, namely, the relation of mythological truth to historical truth; and to this question we must now give some attention. As we do so, the christological myth will still be at the center of our interest, and we shall be asking the question especially in that connection.

As a matter of fact, among the significant biblical myths from the Christian's point of view, it is only the christological myth with respect to which the question arises. Of the other two great myths, one (that of God's creation of the world and man and of the latter's estrangement) belongs to prehistory and the other (that of God's final or eschatological judging and saving action) has to do with what will "happen" after history shall have ended. Only the story of his redemptive, reconciling deed in Christ refers to an actual historical event. W. Norman Pittenger argues that this distinction has such importance that the word "myth," which truly applies in the other cases, should not be used of the christological story. His point is so relevant, not only to the understanding of the nature of myth, but also to the practical purposes of this book that I need both to quote him at some length and (since I have been using "myth" in a way he disallows) to consider seriously the *caveat* he raises. He writes:

The word "myth" does not appear to me to be a satisfactory term to use to describe such events as the Incarnation of God in Christ or the Atonement wrought by him. It is of the nature of "myth" to be descriptive either of ultimate and unique "events," such as the creation of the world or the end of history; or of universal or general truths, such as . . . [that] of man's estrangement from God. The stories of the creation and the consummation of things, as the Bible tells about them, are "myths." . . .

However, the Incarnation of God in Christ and the Atonement wrought by him are in a different category. When we speak of these, we are not talking about things which like the creation and the consummation are "before" or "after" history. Nor are we talking about universal truths. . . . The stories of the Incarnation and the Atonement are tied up with a specific historical event; they have their grounding in something that actually happened in the course of human history; on the one hand, they are not *outside* history, and on the other they are not true of *all* history. They are concerned with what Christians believe was done *in* history and through the factuality of particular historical happenings. . . .

It seems to me quite misleading to put the life of Christ in the same category as the "myth" of creation or to put the redeeming work of Christ in the same category as the "myth" of man's sinfulness. . . . By lumping all these materials together in one category, we may succeed in suggesting that the incarnate life of Christ and his redemptive work are nothing more than types or helpful representations of what is universally true of human experience in relationship with God. Hence we shall seem to deny the particularity of Christ . . . [or] the historical nature of our religion, which concerns itself with what God does in the world for men. It is for these reasons that I should wish to speak of the life of Christ, with all its consequences in history, as the *saga* or *story* of God's supreme and definitive action.[1]

I am usually in such cordial agreement with what this writer says that I do not find it comfortable to differ from him even as regards the appropriate use of a term; and in view of the notorious difficulty of precise definition and of consistent verbal usage in the field of this discussion, I offer my criticisms with caution and not without misgiving. Let me also say at once that I fully recognize the objections to the use of the word "myth" in speaking of the story of Christ—objections based both on the emotional associations of the term and on certain prevalent understandings of its meaning. I wonder, however, whether most of these objections do not apply also to its use in speaking of God's creat-

[1] *The Word Incarnate* (New York: Harper and Brothers, 1959), pp. 39f.

ing of the world and of the final consummation of his redemptive work. Certainly they do to a large extent. And I
should be inclined to think that if we find the word "myth"
unsuitable at one of these points, we should do better to abandon it altogether and employ such a term as "story" in
speaking of the whole range of biblical and credal material
we have been considering.

One must note that Dr. Pittenger speaks of "*saga* or
story." The word "saga" is a term of Icelandic origin denot-
ing an imaginative account of some important figure of the
past, whether historical or legendary; and although this
original usage has been extended, the term still most characteristically refers to a human hero and his deeds. If, then,
by "story" is meant the kind of story designated also by
"saga," it is obvious that this word cannot be used when we
speak of the Creation and the Consummation, for these are
pure acts of God. The question in that case, however, will
be whether "saga" (or "story" in the sense of "saga") can
any more appropriately be used of the Incarnation. As will
soon appear, I do not think it can be. In other words, it
seems to me that although we can refer to all three of these
narratives of divine actions as "stories," we shall not be using
the word in the sense of "saga" in the case of any of them.

Whether, with this understanding, we speak of "stories"
or "myths" would seem to be a matter of no great importance. But whether we can distinguish between the christological story and the other stories in the way Dr. Pittenger
proposes is a more serious question. I am disposed to say we
cannot. I should say we must regard them all as either
"myths" or "stories" or both; and that the fact that one of
them stands in a different relation to what we call history

than the others, while it makes a difference, does not make so much difference—or better perhaps, does not make a difference of such kind—as to require the use of a separate category.

Before advancing some grounds for this opinion, may I state briefly the two reasons why I prefer "myth" to "story" as the definitive term. The first is the fact that "myth" is the term of narrower, more specific meaning. Any narrative may be called a "story"; a myth is a story of a particular kind—the kind to which, certainly in general, narratives about the actions of divine beings specifically belong. The second reason why I prefer the word "myth" is that it carries a connotation of objective truth which the word "story" does not convey. A "story," even a true one (true in the sense of truly representing the nature or quality of reality), may be entirely imaginative and, as an account of an actual happening, may be (even from the point of view of one who accepts and prizes it) entirely false. But, as I have tried to show in earlier chapters, this cannot be said of the myth. A myth must be believed, in order to be for any given person a myth at all, not to say a true myth. In view of the popular understanding of the term, it may seem strange to say that we should call the Christian stories "myths" precisely because we find and hold them to be true. But I believe a sound understanding of the meaning of the term supports such a usage. Time may prove, of course, that, because of long-standing connotations, the term is not salvable for Christian use. In that case, "story" can fill its place. I should still say, however, that "myth" would have been the more exact and the really appropriate term.

Coming now to the more important question whether we

can make the kind of distinction Dr. Pittenger does between the christological myth (or story) and the others, I should like again to make two points. The first is that we may easily exaggerate the difference history makes by overlooking the fact that whereas the Creation and the Consummation are outside history (if by "history" we mean the human thing R. C. Collingwood[2] and others have taught us to see), they are not outside time; and by "time" here I mean the familiar "linear" time to which history belongs. I referred earlier in this discussion to the insistence of Eliade and others that for ancient man, generally speaking, mythical events took place in "mythical time." Such events were not thought of as happening once for all (as, we would say, true events must do) but were "happening" eternally. The impression of an inexorable forward movement in time is an illusion; there is only "the eternal return," the constantly repeated cycle, the endless round. Now, if "myth" and "mythology" should be defined in such a way as necessarily to presuppose this view of time, then we should need to abandon these words in speaking, not only about the Redemption in Christ, but about both of the other biblical stories as well. For, as Eliade recognizes, the ancient Hebrew and, following him, the Christian did not characteristically think of time in this way. "We find affirmed," he writes,

and increasingly accepted, the idea that historical events have a value in themselves, in so far as they are determined by the will of God. This God of the Jewish people is no longer an Oriental divinity, creator of archetypal gestures, but a personality who ceaselessly intervenes in history, who reveals his will through events (invasions, sieges, battles and so on). Historical facts thus

[2] See *The Idea of History* (New York: Oxford University Press, 1946).

become "situations" of man in respect to God, and as such they acquire a religious value that nothing had previously been able to confer on them. It may, then, be said with truth that the Hebrews were the first to discover the meaning of history as the epiphany of God, and this conception, as we should expect, was taken up and amplified in Christianity.[3]

If we limit the application of this new insight to history in the strict sense and suppose that the ancient Hebrew thought of the environment or context of history as being on all sides an atemporal, motionless eternity, we shall find ample ground for separating between the Redemption (which occurred within history), on the one hand, and, on the other, the Creation and Consummation (which lie outside history), whatever terms we may use in designating each category. But I do not believe we are justified in making the limitation. Time extends beyond history at both ends. I should say that from the ancient Hebrew point of view—and from ours too if we really believe these myths or stories—both the Creation and the Consummation are events in the usual sense of actual occurrences. There was a *time* when God brought the ordered cosmos we know into being, and there will be a *time* when he will finally "work his purpose out to its appointed end." The distinctions between prehistory, history, and posthistory, which are fairly clear to us, can hardly have existed for the ancient Hebrew poet or prophet; and even for us, they do not, I believe, imply a denial of the temporal character of the whole. All three of these myths or stories—Creation, Redemption, and Consummation—have to do with *happenings*, past or future. The second of them occurred

---

[3] Mircea Eliade, *Cosmos and History*, tr. Willard R. Trask (New York: Harper and Brothers, 1959), p. 104.

within human history and took place in connection with events of which we have some documentary record; and this makes it unique in many ways. But I do not see that it separates it in kind from the other two.

The second point, closely related to the first, is that to make this separation is to break up, or at least to threaten, the unity of the whole biblical picture of God's dealings with men and thus to place in jeopardy the integrity of each part of it. We have been speaking of three myths or stories; but it would be more accurate to speak of one all-inclusive myth or story, in which each of the three has its place. We have to do, not with three dramas, but with a single drama in three great "acts." In the first "act" God makes man in his image, but man, misusing the freedom God has given him, becomes estranged from his Creator and subject to evil powers he cannot control. In the second "act" God comes into human life in the person of his Son to reconcile and redeem it. Through the suffering of death he overcomes both man's outer enemies and his inner estrangement. The third "act" has to do with the fulfillment of this saving purpose in a new order yet to be consummated. The inner connection, the essential continuity, between the first "act" in this drama and the second are so evident that no argument is needed. One has only to recall that Christ is "the second Adam," the "first-born" of a new "creation." The dependence of the third "act" on the second is quite as unmistakable, as the primitive expectation of Christ's return to initiate the new age will remind us.

The essential unity of the whole great story is wonderfully celebrated in the opening paragraph of the Epistle to the Ephesians:

Blessed be the God and Father of our Lord Jesus Christ, who has blessed us in Christ with every spiritual blessing in the heavenly places, even as he chose us in him before the foundation of the world, that we should be holy and blameless before him. He destined us in love to be his sons through Jesus Christ, according to the purpose of his will, to the praise of his glorious grace which he freely bestowed on us in his Beloved. In him we have redemption through his blood, the forgiveness of our trespasses, according to the riches of his grace which he lavished upon us. For he has made known to us in all wisdom and insight the mystery of his will, according to his purpose which he set forth in Christ as a plan for the fullness of time, to unite all things in him, things in heaven and things on earth.[4]

We may call this whole either "myth" or "story," but we can hardly fail to find it all of a piece.

It may be significant that Dr. Pittenger in the passage I have quoted speaks sometimes of the "Incarnation" and the "Atonement" and sometimes of the "life of Christ." If by the "life of Christ" is meant the actual personal existence of Jesus of Nazareth and his human career, I should surely agree that the term "myth" does not apply. I should have to add, however, that if this "life" is being spoken of objectively—that is, as objectively as it is ever possible to speak of a human life, whether past or present—then I should doubt that the term "story," if that word has symbolic overtones of any kind, would be any more applicable. But if the phrase "life of Christ" refers to the man Jesus, not in some objective and therefore abstract sense, but as he is remembered in the Church, as the wonder of his deeds and words is reflected in

[4] Eph. 1: 3–10.

its Gospels, as his image is carried in its heart—and I know that at the very least this is what Dr. Pittenger means—then I should feel very strongly with him both that "story" (and moreover "story" in the particular sense of "saga") is an appropriate term for it, and also that "myth" would be misleading.

I should agree with him also that the latter word is not proper in references to "all the consequences in history" which the life of Christ has had. I would understand these "consequences" to be, inclusively, the Church—the historical community and all that has been accomplished, and is yet to be accomplished, through it. The fact of the existence of this community does not belong to "myth"—or, for that matter, to "story," as that word is now being used. Without becoming involved in the intricate business of defining "history"—which in its own way is as difficult as the defining of "myth"—we may say that this fact belongs to the same history as does the fact of France or England, and in precisely the same sense. And this is true, not only of the Church's institutional forms, but also of its characteristic inner life—its remembrance of Jesus, its knowledge of his present reality, the reconciliation it knows in thus knowing him. All of this inner experienced meaning belongs to the historical existence of the Church, just as a certain characteristic inner life belongs to the existence of any historical culture. The Church may need myth or story to express the concrete meaning of its existence, and even to apprehend or realize it; but the concrete meaning itself is neither myth nor story. It is the inner reality, the real substance, of the Church's being and belongs to history just as surely as do the external forms of cult and creed. If, then, our attention is focused either on

the "life of Christ" or on its "consequences in history," I
agree with Dr. Pittenger that the word "myth" is unsuitable
and misleading.

But when we speak of the "Incarnation" and the "Atonement," we enter, it seems to me, a quite different world of
discourse—that is, if we are using these terms in their traditional and usual sense. It is true that the concrete reality to
which these words finally point is the same concrete reality
of the Church's life we have been considering. It is the reconciling and healing presence of "the God and Father of our
Lord Jesus Christ"—which means, of God as known in the
community created in and around the person and career of
Jesus of Nazareth. The "Incarnation" is a way of alluding to,
and describing, this realized presence in this particular historical community; and the "Atonement" designates its actual
healing and reconciling character and effect. But although
this is the reality to which these words ultimately point and
which ultimately explains and justifies their use, their meaning in the immediate context is somewhat different. The "Incarnation" refers primarily, or immediately, to the coming of
God into history in the person of his Son and to his dwelling
among us in human form; and the "Atonement," to God's ac-
complishing the annulment of man's guilt and the release
from his bondage through the dying of this same Son on the
cross. In other words, each of these terms refers in the first
instance, not to concrete, experienced reality itself, but to a
dramatic representation of it. They are terms in a story or
myth.

This myth, or story, belongs to history in the sense that it
was created in history and answers to history (namely, to
the life of the historical Church with its remembered, be-

loved and worshiped Lord); but it is not itself history in the sense of being an account of a historical event or development. Moreover, the fact that it utilizes certain data which are historical—that is, some of the facts of Jesus' career—does not make it so. History is made up of the acts and thoughts of men. When we begin talking about *God's* acts and thoughts, even though some of these acts or thoughts are closely associated with historical events, we have entered the world of myth or story. If, in connection with a historical fact, we find ourselves speaking of a deed of God, it is because we are trying to represent and explain the fact's full quality or ultimate meaning. In such a case, the fact belongs to history; even our representation of its meaning belongs to history; but if this representation takes the form of a story of an act of God, that story is, in the nature of the case, not history but myth. This does not mean that it conflicts with history or "intrudes" into history; but, rather, that its essential action takes place outside history entirely, on a different level, in a different realm.

A frequently quoted passage in Kierkegaard begins: "The historical fact that God existed in human form is the essence of the matter; the rest of the historical detail is not even as important as if we had to do with a human being instead of with God."[5] Without presuming to discuss Kierkegaard or even the meaning of this particular passage (which I know only in translation), may I merely lift out the English phrase, "the historical fact that God existed in human form," and ask what we make of it? I submit that we cannot accept it. "That God existed in human form" is not a "historical

[5] *Philosophical Fragments*, tr. David Swenson (Princeton: Princeton University Press, 1936), p. 87; (rev. ed., 1962), p. 130.

fact." The statement is a mythological, not a historical, statement. It refers to a "story," or a dramatization, of a historical event, not to the event itself. We may believe it; but if we do, it will be in the way we believe a myth. We may find it true; but if so, it will be in the way we find a "story" true. We may—I should say, we shall—find it quite impossible to express the quality of the historical fact we are concerned with (namely, the Church's existence) or to explain how it could have come to pass, without saying, and meaning, "God existed, or came to exist, in human form." This statement will be true for us, even historically true in the sense that it will represent the true inwardness of an historical fact. But it is not a bare statement of that fact.

When we say, "Jesus was born about 5 B.C. in Palestine," we are obviously making a historical statement. When we go on to say, "He was good and great beyond what we would have thought possible for man," we are still making a historical statement. But when we say, "He was in the form of God . . . but emptied himself, taking the form of a servant . . . ,"[6] we have entered another world of discourse. Similarly, when we say, "Jesus was crucified under Pontius Pilate," we are making a historical statement. So are we still when we say, "This death became the center of the Church's remembrance of him and the focus of the reconciling meaning it found in him." But when we say, "God showed his love for us in that while we were yet sinners Christ died for us,"[7] our statement is no longer a direct statement of historical fact. It makes contact with the actual occurrence—namely, the death of Jesus—only by way of a dramatization of its realized meaning.

[6] Phil. 2: 6ff. [7] Rom. 5: 8.

In saying, "Christ died for us," we may be thinking of him as meeting the enemy Death in an agonizing, but finally victorious, struggle, thus destroying his power and setting us free. Or we may be thinking of him as paying a debt we owe, or suffering a penalty we have incurred, or offering sacrifice for our sin.[8] But in either case we are not stating the historical fact but are trying to express the meaning that fact has proved to have. This we cannot do without moving beyond the limits of history and confronting the mystery of God's being and action. In such a confrontation either one is silent or one speaks in the terms of story or myth.

[8] These are metaphors within a single basic myth or story and serve to point up the distinction between metaphor and myth. In speaking of the redeeming work of Christ, the New Testament and the literature of devotion use many metaphors; but there are only two myths—this one, in which Christ "atones," and the other, in which he "ransoms" or "liberates."

CHAPTER FIVE

MYTH, LEGEND, AND CREED

W E have seen that a true myth cannot conflict with history for the reason that its essential action takes place outside history entirely—in another realm or at another level than the historical. (This might be added as a fifth "note" to those mentioned at the beginning of Chapter III.) I have tried to show that this historical detachment or transcendence is just as truly characteristic of the myth which seeks to interpret a historical fact (like, say, the life and death of Jesus) as of the myth which does not make contact, so to speak, with history in the strict sense at all (like the myth of Creation). Even the myth which is concerned with the meaning of history does not "compete" with it, or "invade" it, or "intrude" on it. It does not make demands on history. It can take, and at its best wants to take, history as it is, just as the ancient pagan myths at their best were concerned about nature as it is. Faith in Helios or in the glorious

Phoebus was quite compatible with the observation of the sun's invariable movement across the sky, and the ordinary dawn was quite beautiful enough to suggest Aurora's presence. Nothing more "miraculous" than the unfailing wonder of the familiar world was needed to justify, and require, the myths.

I have spoken of "myth at its best," meaning myth in what I am regarding as the true, pure sense. Myth in that sense is interpretative of fact, whether the fact belongs to nature or history. But myth carries in itself the tendency to be also inventive of fact; and when, or insofar as, this tendency is operative, myth moves into the actual sphere of nature or history or onto the same plane, always with confusing, and sometimes with distorting, effect. Instead of telling us what is (or was) really happening, under, in, and through the given facts; it presumes to inform us of new facts. But not only is it incapable of doing this; it ceases to be true myth when it tries. We had occasion to note in an earlier lecture that "not every miracle story is a myth." It would be more accurate to say that no miracle story can properly be called a myth. For the story a miracle story tells is primarily or basically a human story—that is, a story whose essential action occurs in human space and time. Its central interest is in narrating an incident—a supernatural incident, to be sure, but still an actual incident, whether in nature or history. But the story the myth tells moves at a different level; the "incidents" it describes belong neither to history nor to nature although they may often correspond very closely to the unique events of the one and to the constantly recurring features of the other.

The preceding chapter began with some critical comments on W. Norman Pittenger's distinction between "myth" and "story or saga." It may be appropriate to quote —this time with complete approval—what he has to say about another distinction:

Associated with this story or saga [that is, the Incarnation and the Atonement in Christ] there are many tales which have come down to us in the New Testament material which accompanies the story but the nature of which we cannot so readily describe as historical or as based on factual events [nor, as we have seen, do they belong integrally to the story or myth]. . . . In the Old Testament, similar material accompanies the saga of Moses and the exodus. For all of these I should use the word "legends." It is highly unlikely that these stories are in any sense "eye-witness" reports; it is almost certain that they manifest a considerable heightening of the "miraculous" element which is so common in stories told about the "founders" of a religion and about great saints and prophets. . . . It is true that they may contain some elements of genuine history. . . . But they have their principal significance in that they enable us to see what in fact Christ had come to mean to those who believed in him. . . . This is true of the nativity stories, the accounts of the empty tomb, and the Ascension; and it is also true of the stories of Pentecost, which bear their witness to the empowering and enlightening of those who had known Jesus and had experienced the renewal of his presence and power after his ignominious crucifixion, death and burial.[1]

I agree with Dr. Pittenger that such "legends" form a third category. They are neither "history" nor "myth" (or "story"). It is possible, however, that because of the differ-

[1] *The Word Incarnate* (New York: Harper and Brothers, 1959), pp. 40f.

ence he finds between "myth" and "story" he would define the distinction of "legend" somewhat differently from the way I should be disposed to see it. For me the matter can be put, with apparent paradox, in this way: Legends are to be distinguished from history because they are not historical; they are to be distinguished from myth because they are. By their being "not historical" I mean that legends are for the most part not historically accurate and are never historically reliable; they are not history in the sense that they are not *good* history. But their separation from myth is a deeper one. For in another sense they *are* historical. They claim to be, or pretend to be, or want to be. But myth does not. Legends occupy historical space, so to speak; myths do not. Legends can conceivably be proved true or false by historical evidence; myths cannot be.

Because of what was said in the preceding chapter about the close relation in which myth may stand to historical fact, something further may need to be said to justify, or at any rate to clarify, this distinction. If both in legends and in certain myths (especially the Christ myth in its various forms) facts of history, actual or alleged, are involved, how, one may ask, can the distinction between them in this respect be so sharply made? A question of this kind is always ambiguous. It can mean: "Is the distinction a sound one? Is the difference it denotes really there? Do the two categories it seeks to separate really exist?" Or the question may mean: "Can the distinction always be surely drawn? Is there any objective way of determining sharply and with certainty in which of the two categories every particular item of tradition (judged by its relation to history) properly belongs?"

To the latter question one would need to answer No. Although I believe that among those who recognize the propriety of the distinction we are making between "myth" and "legend," there would usually be agreement as to the classification of any given story, one cannot deny that the basis of decision would have been, in large part, certain subjective judgments of value and truth—which means the possibility of both disagreement and error.

But to the other question—the question whether the distinction can *in principle* be made—the answer, I should say, is clearly Yes. There is undoubtedly a difference between a story which came into being to express the inner meaning of a known fact in nature or history and a story which alters, or even invents, the fact itself. In the one case we have a fact creating a story, in the other a story creating a fact. In an earlier chapter I put side by side the story of the Christ (which I called "myth") and the story of the raising of Lazarus (which I would call "legend"). Both involve actual (or alleged) fact. But I should say that in the case of the story of the Christ we start with the actual experienced fact (the Church's existence as a community which remembers Jesus and knows him as Lord) and then find that we cannot apprehend or represent the realized meaning of this fact without the story, whereas in the other case we begin, and end, with the story—a story whose purpose was not so much to explain an already known fact as to inform us of a fact we should otherwise not know. This, I believe, is never the purpose of a myth in the true sense. Certainly it is not true of myth as I have been trying to use the term.

Perhaps an additional example will make the distinction clearer. One form of the myth (or story) of the Incarnation

affirms that the dying of Jesus was *really* the victorious en-
counter of the Christ with man's great enemy Death. Or, as
another form of the story may say it, when Jesus died, God
paid the price of man's redemption. To speak so is, as I see
it, to speak in terms of myth. It is true that the myth stands
in close and necessary relation to an actual historical fact,
namely, the death of Jesus; but it is in no sense or part the
intention of the myth to inform us of it. We *start* with the
fact; the myth neither creates it nor in any way alters it.
Rather, it *interprets* it. It tells what was "really happening"
(in another realm, or on another plane, than the historical)
when this particular historical incident occurred. But consider, in contrast to this story, the stories that when Jesus
died the veil of the temple was rent from top to bottom, that
darkness suddenly settled on the earth and remained from
the sixth to the ninth hour, and that the tombs were opened
and the dead walked the earth again. Here we have accounts,
not of "occurrences" or "transactions" in "the heavenlies"
which represent the real meaning of certain earthly, temporal happenings, but rather accounts of such earthly, temporal happenings themselves. These are "legends." Myths
are related to actual facts, whether of nature or history, in
the other, quite different way.

Because this distinction of myth—what I have called a
"fifth note"—is so often obscured or ignored, with conse-
quent confusion both in our speech and in our thought, I
should like to spell it out a little more fully, although I know
that in doing so I run the risk of laboring the obvious. I shall
speak of it particularly as it applies to two elements in our
tradition—the two elements with respect to which the con-

fusion I speak of has been most frequent and important, namely, the birth narratives and the narratives of the Resurrection.

As for the Nativity stories, most of us, I dare say, will have no trouble in recognizing, and will feel no hesitation about acknowledging, their imaginative, nonfactual character. The angelic annunciations, the heavenly host and the shepherds, the star and the magi—few, if any, of us will believe that these things actually happened so. The reason we deny—or at any rate doubt—their factualness is not that we have decided in advance that such things *could* not have happened (obviously we have no right to such an a priori assurance), but is rather our recognition that we are dealing here with inherently improbable narratives which are supported by very weak and meager evidence. Given all the facts accessible to us, we are almost bound to find these stories more plausibly explained as products of the imagination than as accounts of fact.

Just as surely, however, they are not myths. They do not qualify on several counts—most obviously perhaps because they do not have the cosmic significance and the indispensable character which a true myth must have. One could manage without any of these stories and indeed without all of them. The author of the Fourth Gospel, not to mention the much earlier Mark, manifestly did. But these stories cannot qualify as myth for another reason: they purport to narrate actual incidents which are subject to historical investigation and may conceivably be susceptible of historical validation or disproof. They may be loosely called "mythological" in the sense of depending on, having their origin in, and reminding one of the myth of the Incarnation. But they are no more true myth than they are reliable history, although they may point truly in both directions.

As for the Resurrection narratives, the situation is not essentially different. The story of the Incarnation must, in the nature of the case, tell of God's raising Jesus from the dead and exalting him to a place on his own right hand. To deny the truth of this exaltation of our Lord after his passion would be to deny, not only an essential statement of Christian faith, but also the existential reality of the Christian life itself—the one because the other. The Christian could not possibly bring himself to say, "The Lord Jesus Christ is dead." The statement would involve a self-contradiction. If he is able to say "the Lord Jesus Christ"—I mean, if that phrase has any meaning for him—he simply cannot add "is dead." One's membership in the Church, one's sharing in this corporate existence, involves one's knowing the living reality of the remembered Jesus. The story of God's raising him from the grave to lordship "in the heavenly places" answers to this existential reality.

But this cannot be said of the stories of various human incidents which the tradition associates with the Resurrection. We are told, for example, that when Jesus arose the soldiers guarding his grave were struck down as by a mighty blow. Some women, coming to anoint his body after his burial, are said to have found the tomb empty; and a later story tells of the neat arrangement of the graveclothes within the tomb. Earlier and much more important are the accounts of various visions of the risen Jesus on the part of his disciples. Whether these stories should be called "historical" or "legendary"— and to what extent or in what mixtures or proportions—I shall not venture to say. I feel sure that visions of the living Jesus actually took place, and I see no ground for a categorical denial of the occurrence of the other incidents, although I find it more plausible to attribute them to the growing legend. But whether historical or legendary, none of these items can be said to belong to the category of myth.

This is true for the same reasons mentioned in connection with the birth stories. But it is particularly pertinent to point out here that the very fact that this question—historical or legendary?—can be raised at all puts these stories outside the category of pure myth. The truth of myth, even its objective truth, is not subject to historical or scientific scrutiny. The statement, "God sent his Son into the world to redeem the world," is no more susceptible of historical testing than the statement, "God said, Let there be light, and there was light," is susceptible of scientific testing. When an assertion is of such kind that it can conceivably be validated or refuted by historical or scientific investigation, it is, by that very token, shown to be nonmythological and, for faith, nonessential. This does not mean that myth does not make contact with actual fact. But the actual fact it is concerned with is experienced or existential fact, not scientific or historical fact. The "light" God made is the light we *see*, and the "Son" God sent is the Jesus whom the Church remembers and still knows.

In my remarks about the Nativity stories I refrained from any mention of the Virgin Birth of Jesus, believing that this item in the tradition called for separate comment. I would now express the judgment that this story too fails to qualify as "myth." To be sure, it has been so closely associated with the story of the Incarnation as to have become a symbol of it—for many a seemingly necessary symbol—in a way the other birth stories have not. This fact accounts for its place in the Creeds, although in that connection it is important to recognize that the original significance of this item of tradition, the original reason for its inclusion in the Creeds, was the witness it bears, not merely—and often not chiefly—to the miraculous character of Jesus' birth, but rather to the actuality of it: he was *really born*. He was conceived in a human mother's womb and was born in the way any true man must be. The question most likely to trouble the ancient Christian was not, "How can I believe that Jesus was born of a *virgin?*" but, rather, "How can I believe that the Son of God was *born* at all?" Insofar as there was emphasis upon the Virgin Birth, it was, as likely as not, with a view to making the physical birth itself more credible. Still, the miraculous element was there and was important; and it is not surprising that this affirmation of the extraordinary, the unique, circumstances of Jesus' birth became associated inseparably with the affirmation of the extraordinary, the unique, significance of the whole Event it was thought of as initiating.

The recognition of this important symbolic significance of the credal statement that Jesus was "born of the Virgin Mary"—and for the moment I am thinking, not of her identity, but of her virginal state—must not prevent our seeing its true nature. It may be a statement of actual fact—unprovable, to be sure, since the original testimony on which it might have been based has disappeared, but a fact nevertheless. On the other hand, it may be the product of a process of reflection on the wonder of what has happened within the life of the emerging Church. In the first case it may in a certain sense be called "historical"—although there is no possible way in which we can know or establish it as such. In the second case, it has the character of what we are calling "legend." In neither case, however, is it properly called "myth." Whether history or legend, it refers to a fact or circumstance which lacks both the cosmic significance and the existential validation of the true myth, besides being subject to scientific scrutiny and testing in a way a myth is not.

When we say of the "one Lord Jesus Christ" that he was "the only begotten Son of God, begotten of his Father before all worlds, God of God, Light of Light, Very God of Very God, Begotten, not made, being of one substance with the Father by whom all things were made; Who for us men and our salvation came down from heaven and was incarnate by the Holy Ghost . . . and was made man"—when we say all of this, we are speaking in terms of myth and are, by that same token, speaking what we know to be true. Not only are we saying nothing which conflicts with, or could conceivably conflict with, historical or other objective facts, but we are telling a story of cosmic scope which answers truly, and as precisely as any statement could, to what is given in the Church's existence, namely, the realization that in the Event in which it was born the very reality of God himself entered human life and history and became actually embodied there —the Source, even within human existence itself, of the ultimate life and peace for which man was created. But when in the midst of this story we insert the phrase "of the Virgin Mary," we introduce an element which, though it may have its place and function in the Creed, does not belong essentially to the story. The author of the Fourth Gospel, from which such details are notably absent, has been described as "demythologizing" the "kerygma"; it would be more accurate to say that he "delegendizes" the myth. One who can write, "God sent the Son into the world, not to condemn the world, but that the world might be saved through him," or "God so loved the world that he gave his only Son, that whoever believes in him should not perish but have eternal life"—such a one can scarcely be said to have abandoned or replaced the christological story.

We have been speaking of Mary's virginity. Perhaps a word or two should be said about the significance of her being named at all in the Creed. It was not long after the Church began that Mary herself became an object of veneration and in her own name a symbol of certain values in its life—values which, it is possible, some of us need again to recognize and claim.[2] But surely in the earliest creedal statements the naming of Jesus' Mother, like the mention of Pontius Pilate, points to the conviction of the confessing Christian that the Event whose meaning for him can be expressed only in the story of the Son of God who in love came into the world and as Man shared, with reconciling and saving effect, all our infirmities, even to the suffering of death

[2] Once we recognize the important symbolic significance which Mary came to have, we are in position both to understand the later growth of the saga and properly to evaluate such "new" elements in it as the Immaculate Conception and the Assumption. These dogmas are often referred to as obstacles to unity in the Church. They may well be. Neither of them belonged to the primitive or even to the earliest Catholic tradition; and it will be hard, I believe, to find dogmatic norms acceptable to all Christians which were not clearly established as such in the ancient Church. I should not want to say, however, that even these dogmas constitute insuperable obstacles, provided there can be a general recognition of their symbolic character and the mutual granting of a wide freedom in the interpreting and using of them.

—that this Event really happened, at a given time and place, in and around the career of a particular man. But this Event, which thus happened in human space and time, which in certain vital respects is carried in the memory of the Church and which can to a degree be recovered by historical inquiry— this Event is to be distinguished, although it cannot either in fact or in thought be separated, from the deed of God which was accomplished through it. And the story of the one is a different story—a different kind of story—from the story of the other.

That there was in fact this "deed of God"—that it actually occurred—is an indispensable element of Christian faith. The references in the Creeds to incidents and circumstances of Jesus' career serve to remind us of it and to accent its importance. But although such items are symbols of the Church's conviction in this regard, they are not the ground of it. The Church's assurance of the actuality of the historical Event is an aspect of its own self-knowledge. For the Event in its essential character was nothing other than the Church's own coming into being, and the Church cannot doubt the actuality of its own beginning. The historicity of the Event is an inescapable inference from the historical reality of the Church itself.[3]

Near the beginning of this discussion I said that my primary purpose was the very practical one of seeking to be of

[3] I recognize that the sentences of this paragraph need explication and defense to a degree impossible here. I have tried to provide both in other writings and cannot but refer any interested reader to *Criticism and Faith* (Nashville: Abingdon Press, 1952), pp. 26–41; *The Early Church and the Coming Great Church* (Nashville: Abingdon Press, 1955), pp. 42–82; and *The Church and the Reality of Christ* (New York: Harper and Row, 1962).

some help to the Christian who is being forced to recognize that many of his credal affirmations, many of his theological beliefs, are mythological in character. In pursuit of this purpose I have tried to show that mythology, like every form of human discourse, can in its own appropriate way be true; that this truth, when it is present, partakes of both an existential and a more objective nature; and that from a Christian point of view some myths, whether explicative of nature or history, are in fact thus true. But this is not enough. We need, not only to be rid of the apprehensions and fears which make us loath to acknowledge the mythological to be such, but also so to see the positive values in this acknowledgment that we shall make it gladly and gratefully. I should be unhappy if I could not believe that these values have to some extent emerged in the course of our discussion thus far. But it may be appropriate to conclude this essay with a more explicit reference to several of them.

The first of these—what I shall refer to as "credibility"—may seem at first only another way of alluding to that truth of myth which we have been discussing all the while. Our attention thus far, however, has been focused on the credibility of *myth;* now I have in mind, rather, the credibility of Christian beliefs. Our point has chiefly been that the mythological is not to be rejected on the ground that it cannot be believed; actually, it can be believed and, in the strictest sense, is not mythological unless it is. But more than this can be said, and indeed has been said; namely, that in the area of really vital religious confession only the mythological can be believed. The thoughtful Christian can believe his beliefs only if he recognizes their mythological—or at any rate, their generally symbolical—character. For one, therefore, for whom these beliefs are both true and precious, this recognition is a matter of the greatest importance. I should not be able to stand with the congregation when the Creeds are being spoken or sung and to declare, "I believe . . . ," as I do with full conviction and great joy, if I did not understand in this way the nature of many of the affirmations I am making. If I were required to accept all the language of the Creeds in the same literal way I accept an ordinary statement of fact, I should find them, not only incredible, but also unintelligible.

"But why not?" someone asks. "Why not find them so and then abandon and dismiss them? I can see that you can say Yes to these ancient statements only if you are able to look at them in a symbolical way; but why say Yes to them at all? Why not devise statements to which you can say Yes simply and plainly?" This question leads us beyond the advantage of credibility to a value belonging less to our acknowledgment of myth than to myth itself. This value, too, has been referred to often in the course of this discussion. I shall call it "adequacy." What one wants to say and needs to say cannot be said "simply and plainly." All of us have seen modern "creeds" which, eliminating the mythological or reducing it to a minimum, attempt to make clear affirmations in contemporary terms of what are regarded as the essential Christian ideas, philosophical and ethical. To such a "creed" we may be able to assent easily, but can the Christian be content with it? Does it touch the depths of his existence as a Christian? Does it answer to the concrete reality of the Church's historical life? Does it convey the gospel, which after all is not a system of ideas, but the announcement of a divinely significant Event? I feel sure that we shall find any abstract, indeed any modern, statement inadequate. We need the ancient Creeds with their rich symbolism if we would confess our faith.

We need them, sometimes perhaps in spite of their symbolism, but more often and more deeply because of it. What I mean by the first part of this statement is that we sometimes need the ancient Creeds in spite of the fact that we may not find all of the symbolic terms significant or congenial. For example, someone might wish that "born of the Virgin Mary" or "he descended into hell" were not in the Apostles' Creed. I should say, however, that such a personal or, if you will, characteristically modern reaction to some statement or other in the Creeds does not invalidate the need of them, whether on the part of the individual or his generation. The reason for this is the fact that the Creeds *are* the ancient and Catholic Creeds and have been the vehicles for the confession of the Church's faith throughout its long history and throughout the whole world—so much so that they have become the actual carriers of its distinctive being. If we sense the reality of the historical Church and know ourselves as belonging to it, we shall need these common affirmations and shall find ourselves claiming them as our own, sometimes perhaps in spite of our inability to find some particular symbol significant.

But the second part of the statement is more important. We need the ancient Creeds *because* of their mythological symbolism. This is only saying again that we simply cannot express in abstract or matter-of-fact terms the reality of what it is given us to know in Christ. We may differ with one another as to whether a particular image is more or less significant than another or as to whether this or that image is necessary, but we cannot dispense with symbolic images if we would express our common life or confess our common faith. What the Christian has experienced, however partially and brokenly, and therefore needs to affirm is, in its fullness or at its source, "out of this world"; and the Christian creed which simply asserted the conclusions of common sense or of scientific or philosophical thought, speaking in the same terms and with the same voice, would be vapid, futile, and in the profoundest sense untrue. Only a mythological statement of the Church's faith could be an adequate statement.

This adequacy appears in the myth's ability, not only to express and communicate depths in existence to which neither logical nor matter-of-fact statements could reach, but also to represent something of the manifoldness or richness of existential truth. Earlier in this discussion I made the point that a difference between the mythological and the figurative in general lies in a certain economy in the former. Metaphors can be indefinitely proliferated; myths tend to be definitive and exclusive. Even so, however, myths can be variegated enough to answer to the several sides or aspects of reality as we experience it, just as true portraits of the same person can be diversified enough to represent him in the various characters or moods which belong to him. Logical statements have to be inwardly coherent; ordinary statements of fact have to be consistent among themselves; but mythological statements do not need to agree with one another in order to be true any more than portraits do. To be sure, both the portrait and the statement in order to be true must answer truly to the concrete reality they are presuming to represent; but because this reality is complex and many-sided and inexhaustibly rich, not only may it be said that several different portraits and statements may all be true, but also that more than one portrait or statement may be absolutely required if the reality is to be represented with any adequacy.

Thus, in the New Testament there are several "christologies," several stories of who Christ was and what he did, or, to speak more accurately perhaps, several quite different forms of the same basic story. In one story Christ is Man exalted; in another he is God come down. In one he is the expiating *Victim;* in another he is the emancipating *Victor.* If we were in the position of having to choose from among these stories, to settle on one of them as the only true one, we should be incalculably poorer than we are. To recognize them as mythological symbols is to see that all of them may be true—indeed, that they all *are* true since they answer authentically to what belongs to our being in Christ—and that we can hold and prize them all.

It may finally be said that only if we recognize this symbolic character of all our statements about God and his ways with us can we hope for the ultimate formal unity of the Church. If stories or myths are seen as such, they can be great unifying symbols, not only binding Christians together in a particular generation, but also binding all the generations of Christians together (despite changing thought forms and world views) in the one historical body of Christ. If, on the contrary, the true nature of these biblical and credal materials is not recognized and they are proposed as simple statements of fact or as logical or metaphysical propositions, they become instrumentalities of division, perhaps the most formidable obstacles to the growing unity of the Church. The question is really whether these traditional materials are to be living, relevant, and creative, or dead, meaningless, and divisive. The materials are the same; everything depends on whether their character is truly discerned.

We are living at a time of great hope as regards the possibility of a united Church. Not only are the various Protestant bodies drawing together, but—much more important—there is a growing sense of unity and a developing rapprochement among all Christians, Catholic and Protestant, Eastern and Western. No one will expect the actual realization of one great Church within a generation—or two, or three—but at least we can see the possibility of it as a real possibility, and our hearts rejoice. This "coming Great Church" will be the work of God and we shall be very chary of predicting the conditions of its coming. I should say, however, that of two conditions we can be quite sure: it will not come without a full and universal acceptance of the central biblical and credal symbols, and it will not come without a general acknowledgment of their symbolic nature. Without the acceptance of the symbols the one Church would not be the *Church;* without the acknowledgment of their nature it will never be fully *one.* For the very symbols which alone can unite the church will, if not recognized as symbols, continue most deeply to divide it.

INDEX

Aestheticism, 28 f.
Analogy, 6
Anti-intellectualism, 7 ff.
Assumption of the Virgin Mary, 76
Atonement, the, 45, 52 ff., 58, 61 ff.,
     64, 82
Aurora, 24 f., 28 f., 37 f., 66

Bartsch, H. W., 3, 46
Bultmann, R., 3, 46 ff.
Buttrick, G., 20

Campbell, J., 3 f.
Church, the:
   and intellectuals, 8 ff.
   and myths, 42, 49
   concrete existence of, 33, 41, 44,
        49 f., 60, 75, 77, *et passim*
   unity of, 82 f.
Collingwood, R. C., 56
Copernicus, 8
Creation, the, 31 ff., 52 f., 57 f., 65

Creeds:
   adequacy of, 79 ff.
   and Church's life, 80 ff.
   credibility of, 78 f.
   Nicene, 75
   unifying character of, 82 f.

"Demythologizing," 46 ff.

Eliade, M., 3 f., 26 f., 56 f.
Ephesians, 58 f.
Eschatology, 30 f., 52 ff., 57 f.

Faith:
   and facts or propositions, 9 ff., 15
   and knowledge, 11, 17
   as venture, 11 f., 41
"Fall" of man, 31 f., 52, 58
Fear of truth, 12
Fourth Gospel, the, 42 ff., 71, 75 ff.
Frankfort, H. and H. A., 3, 27
Fuller, R. H., 3, 46

Genesis, 31 f.

God:
  action of, 4 f., 35 f., 45 ff., 62, 64, 77, *et passim*
  and truth, 12 f.
  certainty of, 10, 12, 40 f.
  fear of, 12
  transcendence of, 5 f.

Helios, 37, 65
Henderson, Ian, 46
History:
  and legend, 68 ff.
  and time, 56 f.
  meaning of, 52 ff., 60, 62 ff.

Images, 5, 18 f., 22 f., 30, *et passim*
Immaculate Conception, 76
Incarnation, the, 45, 52 ff., 57 f., 61 ff., 69 f., 74, 82

James, William, 39
Jaspers, K., 43
Jesus, life of, 59 ff., 63, 65, 77
Jones, G. V., 46

Kerygma, the, 46 ff., 76
Kierkegaard, S., 62 f.
Kimmel, W., 43
Kluback, W., 43

Lazarus, the raising of, 42 ff., 69
Legends, 36, 43, 67 ff.
"Life of Christ," 59 ff.

Macquarrie, J., 46
Mark, 71
Millay, Edna St. Vincent, 28 f.

Milner-White, E., 13
Miracle stories, 36, 42 ff., 66 ff.
Myth:
  aesthetic power of, 28 f.
  and "demythologizing," 46 ff.
  and history, 26, 51 ff., 65 f., 73
  and kerygma, 46 ff.
  and legend, 36, 43, 66 ff.
  and "story," 53 ff.
  and "subjectivism," 36 f.
  and symbol, 24, 35 f., 42, 80 ff., *et passim*
  as applicable to Bible, 2 ff., 17, 56 ff.
  as archetype, 25 f., 30, 56
  as distinguished from metaphor, 23 f., 28, 32, 37, 44, 64, 81
  as distinguished from miracle story, 36, 42 ff., 45, 66 ff.
  as "existential-expressive," 24 f., 28, 30 ff.
  as "factually true," 23 ff., 27 ff., 31, 36 f., 55, 78
  as indispensable, 4 ff., 36 ff., 50
  as interpretative, not inventive, 66 ff.
  as "objective-explanatory," 24, 27 f., 30 ff., 48
  as socially created, 24, 35 f., 41
  attitudes toward, 1, 6 f., 78 ff.
  christological, the, 44 ff., 51 ff., 68 ff., 82
  definitions of, 3 f., 18, 25, 34 ff.
  eschatological, the, 30 f., 57
  "exclusiveness" of, 24 f., 37 f., 81
  "notes" of, 35 ff., 65, 70
  of creation, 27, 31 ff., 52 f., 57, 65
  paradoxical character of, 27
  possible in modern world? 28 ff.

Nativity stories, 71 f.
Nicene Creed, 75
Numinous, the, 3 f.

Ogden, S. M., 46

Paul, 32, 63
Philosophy and faith, 8 ff., 15 f.,
    38 f.
Phoebus, 66
Pittenger, W. N., 52 ff., 59 f., 67 ff.
Proteus, 25, 28

Resurrection, the, 44, 72 ff.
Revelation, 9 ff., 12, 15 f.
Robinson, J. A. T., 10

Saga, 54, 60
Saint Joan, 18, 21, 23
Science and faith, 8, 13 ff., 38
Secularization, 8
Shakespeare, 20 f., 23
Shaw, G. B., 18, 21, 23
Streeter, B. H., 22
Swenson, D., 62
Symbol, 24, 36, 42 f., 49, 80 ff., *et
    passim*

Throckmorton, B., 46
Tillich, P., 10, 27, 42 f.
Time:
    and history, 56 f.
    "annulled," 26
    different views of, 3, 26 f., 56 f.
Trask, W., 26, 57
Triton, 25, 28
Truth:
    and myth, 18 ff.
    and necessity, 38 f.
    as objective and subjective, 20 ff.
    criteria of, 18 ff.
    fear of, 9, 12
    of science, 13 ff.
    unity of, 15 f.

Venice, 22
Virgin Birth, the, 73 ff.

Watts, A. W., 3 f.
Whitehead, A. N., 10
Wilde, J. T., 43
Wilder, A. N., 43, 46
Will to believe, the, 39
Wordsworth, 25

MYTH AND TRUTH

was composed and printed
by Connecticut Printers, Inc., Hartford, Connecticut,
for the University Press of Virginia, Charlottesville.
The types used are Linotype Janson
and Janson Display.
The paper is Perkins & Squier RRR
made by the P. H. Gladfelter Company.
Binding is by the Russell-Rutter Company, New York.
The book was designed by John J. Walklet, Jr.